Jane's Patisserie

CELEBRATE!

Jane's Patisserie

CELEBRATE!

BAKE EVERY DAY SPECIAL

JANE DUNN

sourcebooks

Contents

Introduction

Oh, hi there! Welcome to my kitchen.

I'm Jane Dunn, the baker, blogger, foodie, author and general food-obsessed person behind the blog Jane's Patisserie, and I am so excited to be back with another heavenly book of utterly delicious recipes!

For those of you who are new here, I have been running my blog since November 2014 and I love all things baking – cakes, desserts, sweets, cookies, cheesecakes – I will never get bored of creating recipes to share with all of you. Experimenting with new ideas is my number one pastime, whether that's combining iconic flavours with different bakes – like my Black Forest Pavlova (page 162) or Cosy Hot Chocolate Brownies (pages 152–3) – or levelling up a classic bake with my favourite chocolates – like my Mini Egg NYC Cookies (page 130). My recipes are always designed so that novice bakers or those with very little baking experience can get the same results as someone who has baked as much as me.

My blog has grown at an amazing rate – quicker than I ever thought possible – and it's now become one of the biggest food blogs in the country! I've been on such an amazing journey, seeing you all making my recipes and it's a dream come true to have you using my books in real life. For me, there's nothing better than getting your most treasured recipe book covered in ingredients because it means it's been loved, and I adore seeing my books being well-used and getting messy in the same way. My followers are what keep me going and I can't thank you enough for the support you've given me over the years. I'm so excited to bring you the book that you have ALL been waiting for – *Jane's Patisserie: Celebrate!*

I enjoy baking all year round, whatever the season and whatever the celebration. In this book there are SO many opportunities to have fun with your bakes and really raise the bar on every item you rustle up for your friends and family. Covering festive bakes for every possible occasion – **Birthdays, Halloween, Easter, Christmas, Summer BBQs, Valentine's Day** and more – as well as iconic bakes with a twist that will make every day special, this book is packed with tasty celebratory treats.

If you are looking for a bake for a particular occasion I've included a seasonal index at the back of the book to help (see pages 268–9).

As with my first book, I've included classic recipes from my blog – like my **Chocolate Orange Millionaire's Shortbread** (pages 146–7) and my **Raspberry Prosecco Trifle** (page 164) – but I've also listened to my followers' suggestions and made sure that this book is full of the brand new and exclusive recipes that you've requested. The recipes are so varied and hugely enjoyable to make and there is even a chapter on Savoury, Bread and Pastry bakes for those with less of a sweet tooth (pages 238–63). It's difficult to pick my ultimate bakes, but I'd have to include the **No-bake Rainbow Cheesecake** (page 36), **Espresso Martini Cake** (pages 54–5), **Sticky Toffee Muffins** (page 105), **Garlic Stuffed Bread** (page 242) and **Mini Party Sausage Rolls** (page 240).

If you are like me (and most likely if you follow my blog and my books you are!), you will be crazy about baking. Putting together this book has been the best journey and I'm so thrilled with all the recipes. I really hope it gives you pleasure, I'm so proud of it – thank you!

Jane x

LEVELLING UP YOUR BAKING

I adore classic baking, as we all know, and my first book featured a lot of my favourites. My goal with this book is to show you how easy it can be to level up your bakes to create the ultimate homemade treats, suitable for celebrating any occasion or making any day special – and to have fun in the process!

There are a few simple rules when it comes to baking, as results rely on basic chemistry, so I've included a few of my top tips here:

1. Make sure you use the correct ratios when making sponges.

2. When making cheesecakes, be sure to use full-fat soft cheese. You need the right fat content for the cheesecakes to set properly.

3. I use medium eggs for all my recipes, unless otherwise stated.

4. Don't mix up your raising agents. Bicarbonate of soda and baking powder are two different ingredients and should always be used as such.

5. I prefer to use specialist cake decorating colours and I usually find them online. I always recommend using oil-based colours as they react differently to the standard non-oil-based food colourings when mixed with different ingredients. Only oil-based colours should be used when mixing with melted white chocolate, for example.

Get Creative

Many of the recipes in this book have been designed for a specific occasion, but of course they can be made whenever you crave them and I'd always encourage you to experiment and enjoy the creative process.

Simple swaps in colour and decoration can completely change a bake and it's a fun way to make a recipe your own. For example, if you wanted to make my **No-bake Rainbow Cheesecake** (page 36) at Christmas time, you could swap the six rainbow colours for white, red and green! Or if you wanted to make it at Easter, you could mellow out the cake with pastel colours. My **Halloween Sandwich Cookies** (page 128) would work for any other time of year if you change the colours and use different-shaped cutters, depending on your chosen theme.

It's the same with flavours. In a festive recipe I will often use milk chocolate orange, but if you wanted to make the same bake during the spring and summer months, you might like to switch to more of a lemon flavour paired with white chocolate. I hope this little guide will help you with ideas:

Colours

Obviously, you should colour your bakes as you wish, but I always think:

- **VALENTINE'S DAY** = Pink, red, white
- **EASTER** = Pastel purple, pastel pink, pastel yellow, green
- **SUMMER** = Bright colours such as orange, purple, green
- **HALLOWEEN** = Red, orange, black, brown
- **CHRISTMAS** = Red, green, white
- **NEW YEAR'S EVE** = Gold, silver, navy, black
- **BIRTHDAYS** = Bright colours such as blue, purple, pink or the person's favourite colour!

Flavours

- **VALENTINE'S DAY** = Dark chocolate, berries, intense flavours
- **EASTER** = Lemon, carrot, milk chocolate, white chocolate
- **SPRING/SUMMER** = Berries, orange, lemon, apples – all things fruit
- **AUTUMN/HALLOWEEN** = Caramel, toffee, pumpkin, spices
- **CHRISTMAS** = Gingerbread, peppermint, chocolate orange, cinnamon
- **NEW YEAR'S EVE** = Prosecco, champagne, cocktails
- **BIRTHDAYS** = Vanilla, chocolate, anything that is that person's favourite!

Decorating

When it comes to decorating your bakes it is all about practice. I may have trained as a chef when I went to cookery school, but I have learnt a lot through practising over the years since starting my blog. Just remember, everyone has to begin somewhere and you should expect to make mistakes!

Here are my top tips for decorating:

1. When it comes to piping buttercream or whipped cream you can always have a practice first – prep your piping bag and piping nozzle of choice and experiment on a clean plate or a chopping board. You can then scoop the piped filling back into the bag to use on your bake once you have more confidence and also to avoid waste!

2. When it comes to piping a chocolate drip over a drip cake, I always use a small piping bag, with the end snipped off. It's far easier to fill a sealed piping bag and cut 3–4mm off the end to help you easily guide your drip instead of using a nozzle. Aim the piping bag at the top edge of the cake and let the chocolate drip down the sides – the more chocolate you let drip, the longer the drip will be, so vary it each time for a better effect and less of a uniform look.

3. When I am piping icing on cupcakes, I tend to start in the middle of the cupcake and swirl out to the edges of the cake, continuing to swirl upwards to get an ice cream-style look – it's about finding what works for you, so don't worry if you do it a different way!

4. If you're not confident with piping or you'd like to find another way to decorate your bakes, there are an incredible range of sprinkles, edible glitters and cupcake cases or baking cups out there. Search in your local supermarket or online and see what you can find. I love using funfetti sprinkles, which I source online, as they stay bright after baking.

Ingredients

It's always helpful to have a cupboard stocked with your baking essentials and all my recipes use ingredients that you can easily find in your local shops. Other than the essentials such as flours, sugars and fresh ingredients like eggs and butter, there are some ingredients I would also suggest you have to hand when baking for celebrations throughout the year:

OIL-BASED FOOD COLOURINGS SUCH AS:
- Red
- Orange
- Yellow
- Green
- Blue
- Purple
- Black
- White
- Pink

FOOD FLAVOURINGS SUCH AS:
- Vanilla
- Peppermint
- Orange
- Lemon
- Coffee
- Almond

SPICES SUCH AS:
- Ground ginger
- Ground cinnamon
- Nutmeg
- Mixed spice
- Ground cloves
- Garlic
- Chilli flakes
- Mixed herbs
- Smoked paprika
- Chilli powder
- Ground cumin

CHOCOLATES SUCH AS:
- Easter chocolates and chocolate eggs
- Dark chocolate (always 70%+ cocoa content!)
- Milk chocolate
- White chocolate
- Christmas-themed chocolates
- Your favourite chocolates from the confectionery aisle

FRUITS SUCH AS:
- Strawberries
- Raspberries
- Blueberries
- Cherries
- Lemons
- Oranges
- Apples
- Peaches
- Watermelon
- Passion fruit

EXTRAS SUCH AS:
- Brightly coloured sprinkles
- Edible glitters
- Chocolate spreads
- And anything else you fancy...!

Equipment

Just like with the ingredients, you don't need a fully-fitted out kitchen to make my recipes, but there are pieces of equipment I recommend that can really help you along the way, such as food mixers and mixing bowls. Here are some of the items that may be useful:

PIPING NOZZLES

- **2D closed star** – By far my favourite piping nozzle for cupcakes, cakes, whipped cream and more!

- **1M open star** – I love this one for decorating large cakes, or to change it up a bit when piping a cupcake frosting.

- **Jumbo round** – I use this for large cakes usually as the results are so pretty!

- **French piping nozzle** – I often use this for a more detailed effect on a cupcake.

CAKE DECORATING TOOLS

- Small, angled spatula
- Large metal scraper
- Turntable
- Palette knife
- Large piping bags
- Small piping bags
- Piping nozzle coupler

CAKE TINS/TRAYS

- 20cm round cake tins
- 23cm square cake tins
- 23 x 30cm and 23 x 40cm baking trays
- 23cm tart tins
- 900g loaf tin
- 1.5L pudding basin
- 12-hole muffin tray
- Bundt tin
- Trifle bowl
- 8cm pudding moulds
- Dessert glasses or ramekins

EXTRAS SUCH AS:

- Cookie cutters
- Jam jars
- Chocolate moulds
- Tulip muffin cases
- Paper straws
- Mini sparklers
- Colourful cupcake cases or baking cups
- Paper cocktail stick decorations – like mini paper umbrellas

Cheesecakes

NO-BAKE CHOCOLATE HAZELNUT WAFER CHEESECAKE

Cheesecake is sweet, delicious and perfect served as a dessert. This beautiful wafer-topped cheesecake is ever so light and nutty with a crunchy biscuit base – the most important part in my eyes – I love a decent biscuit layer. If you want to make the base even nuttier and more heavenly, add 50g finely ground hazelnuts and 25g more butter. Decorate the cheesecake however you please, but I always think the more you can add the better! Why not make this for a special dinner celebration? It's a crowd-pleaser for kids and adults alike.

SERVES: 12+
PREP: 1 hour
SET: 6+ hours
DECORATE: 30 minutes
LASTS: 3+ days,
in the fridge

Base

100g unsalted butter
300g digestive biscuits

Filling

250g milk chocolate
500g full-fat soft cheese, at room
   temperature
100g icing sugar
1 tsp vanilla extract
300ml double cream
12 chocolate hazelnut filled wafers
   (I use Kinder Bueno), chopped

Decoration

150ml double cream
2 tbsp icing sugar
50g milk chocolate, melted
3–4 chocolate hazelnut filled
   wafers (I use Kinder Bueno),
   chopped
Sprinkles (optional)

Base

Melt the butter in the microwave in short bursts or in a small pan over a medium heat. In a food processor, blitz the biscuits to a fine crumb, add the melted butter and pulse a few times until the mixture is well combined. Press the mixture firmly into the base of a 20cm springform cake tin.

Filling

Melt the milk chocolate in the microwave in short bursts or in a heatproof bowl set over a pan of simmering water (bain-marie) until fully melted. Leave to cool for a few minutes.

In a large bowl, whisk the soft cheese, icing sugar and vanilla extract until combined. Add the melted and cooled chocolate and whisk again until smooth. Pour in the double cream and continue to whisk the mixture until it starts to thicken to a mousse-like texture. (Alternatively, you can whip the cream separately and then fold through the cheesecake/chocolate mix.) Fold the 12 chocolate hazelnut filled wafer pieces through the mixture, if using. Spread the mixture over the biscuit base, smooth over evenly, cover with foil and chill in the fridge for at least 5–6 hours, or preferably overnight.

Decoration

Once chilled, run a knife around the edge of the tin and remove the cheesecake to a serving plate. In a large bowl, whip the double cream and icing sugar together until soft peaks form. Transfer to a piping bag with a piping nozzle fitted. Drizzle the melted chocolate over the cheesecake, pipe over the whipped cream in swirls and add some chocolate hazelnut filled wafer pieces. Scatter over some sprinkles if you fancy.

NO-BAKE LEMON CHEESECAKE

The basic appeal of this cheesecake is that it is insanely easy to make and utterly SCRUMPTIOUS. A delicious shortbread biscuit base, topped with a sharp and lemony filling. I use fresh lemon juice, but this can be substituted for 1–2 teaspoons of lemon extract if you prefer. You can also make it look more 'lemon' themed by adding some yellow food colouring. I love the buttery shortbread base, but you can use digestive biscuits or similar – use 100g melted butter if using a biscuit with less butter content. I would 100% make this cheesecake for a summery party in the garden, or even my dad's birthday!

SERVES: 12+
PREP: 30 minutes
SET: 6+ hours
DECORATE: 30 minutes
LASTS: 3+ days,
in the fridge

Base

85g unsalted butter
300g shortbread biscuits

Filling

600g full-fat soft cheese, at
   room temperature
100g icing sugar
300ml double cream
75ml lemon juice (about
   3 medium lemons)

Decoration

150ml double cream
2 tbsp icing sugar
Lemon slices
Lemon zest

Base

Melt the butter in the microwave in short bursts or in a small pan over a medium heat.

In a food processor, blitz the biscuits to a fine crumb, add the melted butter and pulse a few times until the mixture is well combined. Press the mixture firmly into the base of a 20cm springform cake tin.

Filling

In a large bowl, whisk the soft cheese and icing sugar until combined. Pour in the double cream and continue to whisk the mixture until it starts to thicken to a mousse-like texture. (Alternatively, you can whip the cream separately and then fold through the cheesecake mix.) Add the lemon juice and whisk again.

Spread the mixture over the shortbread biscuit base, smooth over evenly, cover with foil and chill in the fridge for at least 5–6 hours, or preferably overnight.

Decoration

Once chilled, run a knife around the edge of the tin and remove the cheesecake to a serving plate.

In a large bowl, whip the double cream and icing sugar together to form soft peaks. Transfer to a piping bag with a piping nozzle fitted. Pipe the whipped cream in swirls over the cheesecake and add some lemon slices and grated lemon zest.

NO-BAKE GINGERBREAD CHEESECAKE

Can we truly go through the festive period without something fragrant and gingerbread themed? No, no we cannot. I am an absolute gingerbread fiend and I am in love with this No-bake Gingerbread Cheesecake. I use shop-bought gingernut biscuits for the base, but the homemade Gingerbread Biscuits recipe (page 122) from this book works wonderfully as well! I love adding little gingerbread people and some cute sprinkles for decoration, it makes it the best showstopper for the Christmas table. However, if you wanted to make this at any other time of the year, I really wouldn't judge!

SERVES: 12+
PREP: 30 minutes
SET: 6+ hours
DECORATE: 30 minutes
LASTS: 3+ days, in the fridge

Base

90g unsalted butter
300g gingernut biscuits

Filling

750g full-fat soft cheese, at room temperature
75g icing sugar
1 tsp vanilla extract
2 tsp ground ginger
½ tsp ground cinnamon
300ml double cream

Decoration

150ml double cream
2 tbsp icing sugar
Gingerbread cookies
Gingerbread cookie crumbs
Sprinkles

Base

Melt the butter in the microwave in short bursts or in a small pan over a medium heat.

In a food processor, blitz the biscuits to a fine crumb, add the melted butter and pulse a few times until the mixture is well combined. Press the mixture firmly into the base of a 20cm springform cake tin.

Filling

In a large bowl, whisk the soft cheese and icing sugar until combined. Add the vanilla extract, ginger and cinnamon and whisk again until combined. Pour in the double cream and continue to whisk the mixture until it starts to thicken to a mousse-like texture. (Alternatively, you can whip the cream separately and then fold through the cheesecake mix.) Spread the mixture over the biscuit base, smooth over evenly, cover with foil and chill in the fridge for at least 5–6 hours, or preferably overnight.

Decoration

Once chilled, run a knife around the edge of the tin and remove the cheesecake to a serving plate.

In a large bowl, whip the double cream and icing sugar together to form soft peaks. Transfer to a piping bag with a piping nozzle fitted and pipe the whipped cream in swirls over the cheesecake. Add a gingerbread cookie to each cream swirl and sprinkle over some crushed gingerbread cookie crumbs and sprinkles.

NO-BAKE STRAWBERRY MILKSHAKE CHEESECAKE

Milkshake is one of those things that I absolutely adored when I was younger and a treat I especially loved during the summer. I mean, how could you not? A creamy ice-cold flavoured milkshake is ideal on a hot day or even if you are at a party. The best flavour though? Strawberry. There is something about a strawberry milkshake that is utterly iconic and in cheesecake form it is SO good! You can of course use whatever flavour milkshake powder you like and decorate accordingly – vanilla, chocolate and banana work well too. I've made this several times for family BBQs and it's always a hit.

SERVES: 12+
PREP: 30 minutes
SET: 6+ hours
DECORATE: 30 minutes
LASTS: 3+ days, in the fridge

Base

100g unsalted butter
300g digestive biscuits

Filling

750g full-fat soft cheese, at room temperature
75g strawberry milkshake powder
1 tsp vanilla extract
300ml double cream

Decoration

150ml double cream
2 tbsp icing sugar
12 fresh strawberries
10g freeze-dried strawberries

Base

Melt the butter in the microwave in short bursts or in a small pan over a medium heat.

In a food processor, blitz the biscuits to a fine crumb, add the melted butter and pulse a few times until the mixture is well combined. Press the mixture firmly into the base of a 20cm springform cake tin.

Filling

In a large bowl, whisk the soft cheese, strawberry milkshake powder and vanilla extract until combined. Pour in the double cream and continue to whisk the mixture until it starts to thicken to a mousse-like texture. (Alternatively, you can whip the cream separately and then fold through the cheesecake mix.)

Spread the mixture over the biscuit base, smooth over evenly, cover with foil and chill in the fridge for at least 5–6 hours, or preferably overnight.

Decoration

Once chilled, run a knife around the edge of the tin and remove the cheesecake to a serving plate.

In a large bowl, whip the double cream and icing sugar together to form soft peaks. Transfer to a piping bag with a piping nozzle fitted. Pipe over swirls of the whipped cream and add a strawberry to each piped swirl. Sprinkle over the freeze-dried strawberries.

NO-BAKE CHEESECAKE
FOR TWO

When it's Valentine's Day, you want something simple and luscious to make for dessert and this is the one. A quick biscuit base, chocolate cheesecake filling and some romantic chocolate-dipped strawberries to spoil your loved one. You can make these individual cheesecakes vanilla-flavoured by leaving out the cocoa powder or you can even make them caramel-flavoured by swapping the cocoa powder for 35g caramel sauce. Even if you don't want to impress that special someone and you just want to make a dessert for a couple of friends, this recipe is perfect for that too. Double the quantities for four, triple it for six... you get the idea.

SERVES: 2
PREP: 20 minutes
SET: 1+ hours
DECORATE: 15 minutes
LASTS: 3+ days,
in the fridge

Base

30g unsalted butter
60g digestive biscuits

Filling

100g full-fat soft cheese, at room
  temperature
½ tsp vanilla extract
1 tbsp icing sugar
50ml double cream
25g cocoa powder

Decoration

White chocolate-coated
  strawberries
Chocolate curls

Base

Melt the butter in the microwave in short bursts or in a small pan over a medium heat. In a food processor, blitz the biscuits to a fine crumb, add the melted butter and pulse a few times until the mixture is well combined. Divide the biscuit mixture between two glasses and press the mixture down.

Filling

In a large bowl, whisk the soft cheese, vanilla extract and icing sugar until smooth. Add the double cream and cocoa powder and whisk again until smooth and thickened. Spoon the mix equally into the two glasses, and level carefully. Chill in the fridge for an hour or so until set.

Decoration

Decorate with whatever ingredients you fancy – I used white-chocolate-coated strawberries and chocolate curls but crushed-up biscuit crumbs or toasted nuts would also be delicious.

NO-BAKE TOFFEE NUT CHEESECAKE

I wanted to share a combination of flavours with this divine recipe... the sweetness of toffee with the toasted flavour of all things nutty. I used macadamia nuts, as to me they are the 'toffee nut', but the wonderful thing about this recipe is that you can use whatever nut you like. Pecans, walnuts, pistachios and hazelnuts will all work wonderfully! I made a homemade toffee sauce, but you can use shop-bought if you are short on time. A pinch of sea salt mixed into the sauce is a perfect addition to battle the sweet edge. This is a cheesecake that I would make at any time of year, for any celebration or just for a nice treat – I would even serve it at a dinner party!

SERVES: 12+
PREP: 30 minutes
SET: 6+ hours
DECORATE: 30 minutes
LASTS: 3+ days,
in the fridge

Sauce

75g unsalted butter
75g soft dark brown sugar
2 tbsp black treacle
1 tsp vanilla extract
225ml double cream

Base

125g unsalted butter
250g digestives biscuits
100g macadamia nuts

Filling

600g full-fat soft cheese, at room
  temperature
75g icing sugar
1 tsp vanilla extract
75ml toffee sauce (above)
250ml double cream

Sauce

Put all of the ingredients into a large pan and heat over a low-medium heat, stirring all the time until the sugar has dissolved and the butter has melted. Bring the sauce to the boil and continue to stir for a couple of minutes until the mixture thickens slightly. Leave to cool fully, stirring occasionally to stop a skin forming on the sauce as it cools.

Base

Melt the butter in the microwave in short bursts or in a small pan over a medium heat. In a food processor, blitz the biscuits and macadamia nuts to a fine crumb, add the melted butter and pulse a few times until the mixture is well combined. Press the mixture firmly into the base of a 20cm springform cake tin.

Filling

In a large bowl, whisk the soft cheese, icing sugar, vanilla extract and 75ml of the toffee sauce until combined. Pour in the double cream and continue to whisk the mixture until it starts to thicken to a mousse-like texture. (Alternatively, you can whip the cream separately and then fold through the cheesecake mix.) Spread the mixture over the biscuit base, smooth over evenly, cover with foil and chill in the fridge for at least 5–6 hours, or preferably overnight.

Decoration

150ml double cream

2 tbsp icing sugar

Toffee sauce (opposite)

Macadamia nuts, chopped

Decoration

Once chilled, run a knife around the edge of the tin and remove the cheesecake to a serving plate. In a large bowl, whip the double cream with the icing sugar to form soft peaks. Transfer to a piping bag with a piping nozzle fitted and pipe swirls over the cheesecake. Drizzle the cheesecake with some extra toffee sauce and sprinkle over some chopped macadamia nuts. Serve any leftover toffee sauce alongside the cheesecake.

LEMON BLUEBERRY CHEESECAKE BARS

I adore a classically round cheesecake as you might have guessed by now, but do you know what I also love? A cheesecake bar. A beautiful baked cheesecake with a light, heavenly lemon flavour, dotted with blueberries that tastes and looks extraordinary. Cheesecake bars are by far one of the best desserts you can make for a birthday party or any time you want to celebrate. Have fun with the flavours and top the bars with other berries like raspberries or strawberries or switch the lemon zest for orange or lime. I reckon a cranberry version would be wonderful for Christmas too.

SERVES: 12+
PREP: 30 minutes
BAKE: 1 hour
COOL: 6+ hours
LASTS: 3+ days, in the fridge

Base

175g unsalted butter
400g digestive biscuits

Filling

750g full-fat soft cheese
4 eggs
225g caster sugar
2 tbsp cornflour
75g soured cream/natural
  yoghurt
Zest of 2 lemons
250g blueberries

Base

Preheat the oven to 200°C/180°C fan and line a 23 x 33cm rectangular tin with parchment paper.

Melt the butter in the microwave in short bursts or in a small pan over a medium heat. In a food processor, blitz the biscuits to a fine crumb, add the melted butter and pulse a few times until the mixture is well combined. Press the mixture firmly into the base of the tin.

Bake the base in the oven for 10 minutes, then remove the tin from the oven and leave to cool a little.

Filling

Reduce the oven temperature to 160°C/140°C fan.

Add the soft cheese to a large bowl and briefly mix to loosen it. Add the eggs, one at a time, mixing well after each addition (I use a spatula to do this). Add the sugar and cornflour and mix carefully to combine. Finally, add the soured cream, lemon zest and blueberries. Transfer to the tin with the prepared biscuit base.

Bake in the oven for 55–60+ minutes, or until the edges of the cheesecake start to turn golden and the middle retains a slight wobble. Cool in the tin in the oven, with the oven door slightly ajar.

Cover the cheesecake with foil and chill in the fridge for at least 5–6 hours, or preferably overnight. Once chilled, use the edges of the parchment paper to remove the cheesecake to a chopping board and then cut into 12 bars with a sharp knife.

NO-BAKE RAINBOW CHEESECAKE

Who can honestly resist something this beautiful? This gorgeous rainbow cheesecake says 'summer' to me, but it is ideal for any celebration. I used the main six colours (yes, I know there are technically seven colours in a rainbow, but baking with six is far easier!). Feel free to use whatever colours you prefer – pastels, brights or use fewer colours in any combination. Different themes could determine your colour choice – Christmas, Halloween – you decide. I used a vanilla cheesecake base so that the colours really popped, but a different flavouring such as orange, lemon or even peppermint would taste great.

SERVES: 12+
PREP: 30 minutes
SET: 6+ hours
DECORATE: 30 minutes
LASTS: 3+ days, in the fridge

Base

100g unsalted butter
300g digestive biscuits

Filling

750g full-fat soft cheese, at room temperature
75g icing sugar
1 tsp vanilla extract
300ml double cream
Red, orange, yellow, green, blue and purple food colourings

Decoration

150ml double cream
2 tbsp icing sugar
Sprinkles (I use rainbow-coloured sprinkles)

Base

Melt the unsalted butter in the microwave in short bursts or in a small pan over a medium heat. In a food processor, blitz the biscuits to a fine crumb, add the melted butter and pulse a few times until the mixture is well combined. Press the mixture firmly into the base of a 20cm springform cake tin.

Filling

In a large bowl, whisk the soft cheese, icing sugar and vanilla extract until combined. Pour in the double cream and continue to whisk the mixture until it starts to thicken to a mousse-like texture. (Alternatively, you can whip the cream separately and then fold through the cheesecake mix.)

Divide the mixture between six small bowls. Add ¼–½ teaspoon of food colouring to each bowl and stir carefully to colour. Spread the first colour mix over the biscuit base carefully and smooth it evenly. Freeze the cheesecake for 5 minutes to 'set' the first colour layer. Add the second colour mix layer and freeze to 'set'. Repeat until all the coloured layers have been added. Cover the cheesecake with foil and chill in the fridge for at least 5–6 hours, or preferably overnight.

Decoration

Once chilled, run a knife around the edge of the tin and remove the cheesecake to a serving plate. In a large bowl, whisk the double cream and icing sugar together to form soft peaks. Transfer to a piping bag with a piping nozzle attached. Pipe over the whipped cream in swirls. Scatter over your choice of sprinkles!

NO-BAKE CHEESECAKE EGGS

When chocolate Easter eggs are so easy and cheap to buy you can really have some fun experimenting with this recipe. Why not take half of an Easter egg shell, fill it with a biscuit base (carefully – don't go breaking that chocolate), and top with a silky-smooth cheesecake filling? You can decorate with any of your favourite Easter treats too – let's just appreciate how good they look for a second because YUM! You can have so much fun playing with the flavours, with the Easter chocolates you add on top, or even the biscuit flavours in the base. Add 15g cocoa powder to the biscuits for a chocolate base or add 1 teaspoon of orange extract to the cheesecake filling. Also, if you are prepared, these would make great little Easter gifts!

SERVES: 2
PREP: 20 minutes
SET: 1+ hours
DECORATE: 15 minutes
LASTS: 3+ days, in the fridge

Base

1 medium Easter egg
35g unsalted butter
75g digestive biscuits

Filling

200g full-fat soft cheese, at room temperature
½ tsp vanilla extract
2 tbsp icing sugar
100ml double cream
25g cocoa powder

Decoration

50g milk chocolate, melted
Easter chocolates
Sprinkles

Base

Carefully split the Easter egg into two halves.

Melt the butter in the microwave in short bursts or in a small pan over a medium heat. In a food processor, blitz the biscuits to a fine crumb, add the melted butter and pulse a few times until the mixture is well combined.

Divide the mixture equally between the two halves of the Easter egg, and very gently press down, without breaking the shell.

Filling

In a large bowl, whisk the soft cheese, vanilla extract and icing sugar until smooth. Add the double cream and cocoa powder and whisk again until smooth and thickened. Divide the mixture evenly between the two Easter egg halves and smooth over as carefully as possible. Chill in the fridge for an hour or so until set.

Decoration

Drizzle the melted milk chocolate over the two halves and decorate with some Easter chocolates and sprinkles.

NO-BAKE
GRAVEYARD CHEESECAKE

Are we all creeped out by this frighteningly scare-tastic cheesecake? Halloween is such a fun time of year because there are so many goodies about for decorating and creating a ghoulish yet yummy bake, and this is the epitome of that. Using a homemade shortbread to create a black-coloured base, the biscuit crumb dirt and the 'RIP' biscuits was fun, but you can use a different base biscuit if you prefer. Any chocolate biscuits work well for crumbling or use cookies and cream biscuits (I use Oreos) for extra flavour. You can even use shop-bought biscuits to spell out the 'RIP' if you want to make it a little easier. Use whatever delicious gummies you like for the creatures – just have fun with this spook-tacular bake!

SERVES: 12+
PREP: 1½ hours
BAKE: 18–21 minutes
SET: 6+ hours
DECORATE: 30 minutes
LASTS: 3+ days,
in the fridge

Shortbread Biscuits

400g unsalted butter, at room
  temperature
200g caster sugar
600g plain flour, plus extra for
  dusting
1–2 tsp black food colouring

Base

90g unsalted butter
300g black shortbread biscuits
  (above)

Filling

250g dark chocolate
500g full-fat soft cheese, at room
  temperature
75g icing sugar

see next page

Shortbread Biscuits

In a large bowl, cream the butter and sugar together until smooth and fluffy. Add the flour and black food colouring and mix to combine.

Turn the dough out onto a lightly floured work surface and roll out to 1cm thick. Cut out rectangles 6–7cm long and transfer to two or three lined large baking trays. Chill the dough in the fridge for 30 minutes.

Meanwhile, preheat the oven to 180°C/160°C fan. After 30 minutes of chilling, put the trays in the oven and bake for 18–21 minutes. Leave the biscuits to cool fully on the trays.

Base

Melt the butter in the microwave in short bursts or in a small pan over a medium heat. In a food processor, blitz 300g of the shortbread you made earlier to a fine crumb, add the melted butter, and pulse a few times until the mixture is well combined. Press the mixture firmly into the base of a 20cm springform cake tin.

Filling

Add the dark chocolate to a small heatproof bowl and microwave in short bursts or set the bowl over a pan of simmering water (bain-marie) until smooth. Leave to cool.

In a large bowl, whisk the soft cheese, icing sugar and vanilla extract until combined. Add the cooled dark chocolate and fold in until smooth. Pour in the double cream and continue to whisk

1 tsp vanilla extract
300ml double cream
100g black shortbread biscuits
  (above)

Decoration

Black shortbread biscuits
Writing icing tubes or melted
  white chocolate
Gummy worms

the mixture until it starts to thicken to a mousse-like texture. (Alternatively, you can whip the cream separately and then fold through the cheesecake mix.)

Spread the mixture over the biscuit base. Blitz 100g of the shortbread you made earlier in a food processor to a fine crumb. Sprinkle the biscuit crumbs over the cheesecake mixture, pressing down gently.

Cover the cheesecake with foil and chill in the fridge for at least 5–6 hours, or preferably overnight.

Decoration

Once chilled, run a knife around the edge of the tin and remove the cheesecake to a serving plate. With the leftover shortbread biscuits you made earlier, spell out 'RIP' on the cheesecake or decorate them to look like gravestones using writing icing tubes or melted white chocolate.

Carefully decorate the top of the cheesecake with gummy worms, black shortbread biscuits or any other spooky toppings you fancy.

NO-BAKE TRIPLE CHOCOLATE CHEESECAKE

I love chocolate more than most things – and when you combine dark, milk and white chocolate all in one bake (or no-bake!) I am in heaven. You taste the ever so slightly deep and bitter flavour of the dark chocolate, the middle ground from the milk chocolate and the increased sweetness from the white chocolate in every bite – what could be better? You can of course make this an all-dark chocolate cheesecake, or only use two types of chocolate, but just be sure to use the same total weight and split accordingly. This extra indulgent bake could even replace a birthday cake if you wanted to try something completely different!

SERVES: 12+
PREP: 1 hour
SET: 6+ hours
DECORATE: 30 minutes
LASTS: 3+ days,
in the fridge

Base

100g unsalted butter
300g digestive biscuits

Filling

100g dark chocolate
100g milk chocolate
100g white chocolate
600g full-fat soft cheese, at room
  temperature
125g icing sugar
1 tsp vanilla extract
300ml double cream

see next page

Base

Melt the butter in the microwave in short bursts or in a small pan over a medium heat.

In a food processor, blitz the biscuits to a fine crumb, add the melted butter and pulse a few times until the mixture is well combined. Press the mixture firmly into the base of a 20cm springform cake tin.

Filling

Using three different small bowls, add each chocolate type to a bowl. Melt each bowl of chocolate carefully in short bursts in the microwave or set the bowl over a pan of simmering water (bain-marie) until smooth. Leave to cool for a few minutes.

In a large bowl, whisk the soft cheese, icing sugar and vanilla extract until combined. Pour in the double cream and continue to whisk the mixture until it starts to thicken to a mousse-like texture. (Alternatively, you can whip the cream separately and then fold through the cheesecake mix.)

Divide the cheesecake mix evenly between three clean bowls. Add the cooled dark chocolate to one bowl, the cooled milk chocolate to another bowl and the cooled white chocolate to the remaining bowl. Fold the chocolate and cheesecake mix to combine in each of the bowls.

50g dark/milk/white chocolate
150ml double cream
2 tbsp icing sugar
Chocolate curls

Spread the dark chocolate mixture over the biscuit base first, smoothing over evenly. Then add the milk chocolate mixture and smooth over. Finally, add the white chocolate mixture and smooth over. Cover the cheesecake with foil and chill in the fridge for at least 5–6 hours, or preferably overnight.

Decoration

Once chilled, run a knife around the edge of the tin and remove the cheesecake to a serving plate.

Carefully melt 50g chocolate of your choice, in a microwave or a bain-marie, until smooth. Drizzle over the cheesecake.

In a large bowl, whip the double cream and icing sugar together to form soft peaks. Transfer to a piping bag with a piping nozzle fitted. Pipe the whipped cream in swirls over the cheesecake, and sprinkle over the chocolate curls.

Cakes

ETON MESS CAKE

During the summer months I still crave cake, but I usually want something light and easy to make and this is the perfect celebration bake. Eton Mess in cake form is something that's hard to dislike! The sponges are studded with strawberries to bring some moisture to the cake and it has a wonderful airy texture. Add freshly whipped cream, crushed meringues and some jam and you have the ultimate dessert. If you want to mix it up a little, use a different flavour jam, or even a different berry in the cake.

SERVES: 12+
PREP: 30 minutes
BAKE: 25–30 minutes
COOL: 2 hours
DECORATE: 1 hour
LASTS: 2–3+ days,
in the fridge

300g unsalted butter, at room
   temperature
300g caster sugar
300g self-raising flour
6 eggs
300g fresh strawberries, chopped

Decoration

450ml double cream
75g icing sugar
2–4 tbsp strawberry jam
6 meringue nests
12 fresh strawberries
10g freeze-dried strawberries

Preheat the oven to 180°C/160°C fan and line three 20cm springform cake tins with parchment paper.

Add the butter, sugar, flour and eggs to a large bowl and beat until the mixture is smooth. Divide the mixture evenly between the three tins. Lay the strawberries on the tops of the cakes

Put the cakes into the oven and bake for 25–30 minutes. The strawberries create more moisture in the cake batter, so it can sometimes take a little longer to bake. Keep an eye on the sponges – a cocktail stick or skewer inserted into the middle of the cakes should come out clean when the cakes are ready.

Leave to cool in the tins for about 30 minutes, then turn out onto a wire rack to cool fully.

Decoration

In a large bowl, whip the double cream with the icing sugar to form soft peaks.

Spread a tablespoon or two of jam onto the first cooled sponge, and crush over some meringue. Spoon over one-third of the whipped cream and spread as evenly as possible. Add the second sponge layer and repeat. Finally, add the third sponge layer and slather on the remaining cream. Add the fresh strawberries, crumble over the remaining crushed meringue, and finish with a sprinkling of freeze-dried strawberries.

LEMON DRIZZLE LOAF CAKE

I love a classic bake and I am pretty sure my Lemon Drizzle Loaf Cake is the ultimate in its field. It happens to be one of my mum's favourite things to order when she's at a coffee shop and this is my go-to when I want to bake something to brighten her day. I always think gifting something edible, especially if it is homemade, is one of the best presents you can give and this bake is ideal for that. I can't get enough of the lemon icing drizzled over the top, but you can easily substitute it for a lovely lemon-flavoured buttercream or even a soft cheese frosting. Why not combine some yummy flavours and make a lemon-lime drizzle cake?

SERVES: 10+
PREP: 30 minutes
BAKE: 55–65 minutes
COOL: 2 hours
DECORATE: 15 minutes
LASTS: 2–3+ days,
in the fridge

250g unsalted butter, at room
   temperature, plus extra for
   greasing
250g caster sugar
250g self-raising flour
5 eggs
Zest of 2 lemons

Drizzle
75ml lemon juice
75g caster sugar

Decoration
50g icing sugar
1–2 tsp lemon juice
Lemon zest

Preheat the oven to 180°C/160°C fan and grease and line a 900g loaf tin with parchment paper.

In a large bowl, cream the butter and sugar together until light and fluffy. Add the flour, eggs and lemon zest and beat again until well combined and smooth.

Transfer the mixture to the loaf tin and bake for 55–65 minutes, but check from 50 minutes onwards as oven temperatures differ. The cake is ready when a cocktail stick or skewer inserted into the middle comes out clean.

Drizzle
Towards the end of the baking time, put the lemon juice and sugar in a small bowl and mix well. Carefully drizzle the lemon and sugar mixture over the warm cake, while still in its tin. Let the cake cool fully before removing from the tin.

Decoration
Put the icing sugar in a small bowl and gradually add the lemon juice until you reach your desired consistency – the less lemon you add, the thicker the icing. Drizzle over the cake and finally sprinkle over some lemon zest for decoration.

PEACH RASPBERRY CAKE

When I bake a cake with fruit, I always expect something fresh and delicious and this cake 100% represents that – the perfect summery, fruity cake. Using peach slices and raspberries makes for such a light, beautiful bake, especially when you drizzle the juice from the tinned peaches onto the sponge to soak up all that lovely flavour. If you want to use fresh peaches when they are in season, absolutely go for it! You can also use fresh or frozen raspberries. Imagine serving this cake with some custard, or even a scoop of ice cream on a sunny day... oh my.

SERVES: 18+
PREP: 20 minutes
BAKE: 45–50 minutes
COOL: 1+ hours
LASTS: 2–3+ days, in the fridge

325g unsalted butter, at room temperature
325g caster sugar, plus 75g for sprinkling
5 eggs
1 tsp vanilla extract
350g plain flour
1 tsp baking powder
2 x 400g tins sliced peaches
250g fresh/frozen raspberries

Preheat the oven to 180°C/160°C fan and line a 22 x 33cm traybake tin with parchment paper.

In a large bowl, cream the butter and sugar together until light and fluffy. Add the eggs, vanilla extract, flour and baking powder, then beat again until smooth.

When removing the sliced peaches from their tins, reserve the syrup for later. Carefully lay the slices on the bottom of the lined tin, filling in any gaps with the raspberries. Sprinkle over the extra caster sugar.

Carefully spread the cake mixture over the top of the fruit and transfer the cake to the oven to bake for 45–50 minutes until the cake springs back when you press it with your finger.

Leave the cake to cool in the tin for 30 minutes and then carefully turn the cake out onto a serving plate, and remove the parchment paper. The fruit should now be at the top of the cake.

Drizzle the reserved syrup from the sliced peaches over the cake and leave the cake to cool fully before serving.

ESPRESSO MARTINI CAKE

Have you ever thought about merging one of your favourite cocktails into cake form?
How about a three-layer insane showstopper of a cocktail cake? Because this is it for me.
An espresso martini is one of my favourite coffee-based drinks and coffee liqueur and vodka
flavours translate so well into this cake. A coffee-chocolate sponge, soaked with a beautiful
espresso-martini-style drizzle, topped with a tempting espresso-martini-flavoured soft
cheese frosting – can you get any more indulgent than that? This is the sort of bake
I would make for a friend's birthday or even a New Year's Eve party.

SERVES: 15+
PREP: 30 minutes
BAKE: 35–40 minutes
COOL: 2 hours
DECORATE: 1–2 hours
LASTS: 2–3+ days,
in the fridge

400g unsalted butter, at room
temperature, plus extra for
greasing
400g soft dark brown sugar
350g self-raising flour
50g cocoa powder
8 eggs
1 tbsp instant coffee (dissolved in
2 tbsp water)
50ml coffee liqueur

Drizzle
100ml coffee liqueur
75ml vodka
50g soft dark brown sugar

Frosting
250g unsalted butter, at room
temperature
250g icing sugar

Preheat the oven to 180°C/160°C fan and grease and line three
20cm springform cake tins with parchment paper.

In a large bowl, cream the butter and sugar together for
3–4 minutes until light and fluffy. Add the flour, cocoa powder,
eggs, instant coffee and coffee liqueur and beat again for a couple
of minutes until smooth.

Divide the mixture between the three tins and bake in the oven for
35–40 minutes, or until a cocktail stick or skewer inserted into the
middle of the cakes comes out clean.

Drizzle

Pour the coffee liqueur, vodka and sugar into a small pan. Heat over
a low heat, stirring until the sugar has dissolved.

While the still hot cakes are cooling in their tins, gently pour the
coffee drizzle over the cakes, reserving 2–3 tablespoons of
mixture for later.

Leave the cakes to cool fully in the tins.

Frosting

In a large bowl, beat the butter on its own for 3–4 minutes to
loosen it. Add the icing sugar and beat to fully combine. Add the
mascarpone to the mixture and beat again until smooth. Gradually
add the reserved coffee drizzle, 1 tablespoon at a time, beating fully
after each addition.

500g mascarpone, at room temperature
2–3 tbsp coffee drizzle (opposite)

Decoration

Cocoa powder, for dusting
Chocolate-coated coffee beans

Decoration

Lay the first sponge layer on a serving plate or a cake stand. Transfer the frosting to a piping bag with a piping nozzle fitted and pipe one-third of the frosting over the first layer. Repeat with the second and third sponge layers.

Sprinkle over a dusting of cocoa powder and decorate with some chocolate-coated coffee beans.

CARROT WALNUT LOAF

I'm not lying when I say that I think carrot cake is always a winner – there is just something about its savoury sweetness. This cake absolutely levels up the loaf cake game, with the addition of loads of toasted walnuts folded through the sponge mixture, topped with a spiced soft cheese frosting and sprinkled with even more toasted walnuts. If you don't like walnuts, you could use pecans, but don't leave out the nuts! They make this beautifully nutty carrot loaf taste UNREAL and you will love every mouthful.

SERVES: 10+
PREP: 30 minutes
BAKE: 70+ minutes
COOL: 2 hours
DECORATE: 1 hour
LASTS: 2–3+ days, in the fridge

400g walnuts
175ml sunflower oil/vegetable oil, plus extra for greasing
4 eggs
200g soft light brown sugar
250g carrots, grated
200g self-raising flour
1 tsp bicarbonate of soda
2 tsp mixed spice

Frosting

125g unsalted butter, at room temperature
125g icing sugar
1 tsp vanilla extract
½ tsp mixed spice
250g full-fat soft cheese

Preheat the oven to 180°C/160°C fan and line a large baking tray with parchment paper. Scatter the walnuts over the lined tray and bake in the oven for 8–10 minutes, or until they have turned golden.

Leave to cool fully on the tray. Reserve 150g of the toasted walnuts in a bowl and very finely chop the remaining walnuts and leave to one side. Keep the oven at 180°C/160°C fan. Grease and line a 900g loaf tin.

In a large bowl, pour the oil and add the eggs and soft light brown sugar. Lightly mix to combine. Add the grated carrots and the reserved finely chopped walnuts and fold through to combine. Add the flour, bicarbonate of soda and mixed spice and stir again, being careful not to overmix.

Transfer the mixture to the loaf tin and bake in the oven for 55–60 minutes. Oven temperatures vary, so it can take a little longer. Use a cocktail stick or skewer inserted in the middle of the cake and if it comes out clean, the cake is ready. Leave to cool in the tin for 10 minutes, then turn out onto a wire rack to cool fully.

Frosting

In a large bowl, beat the butter for a few minutes to loosen it. Beat in the icing sugar for about 5 minutes until really smooth. Add the vanilla extract and mixed spice and briefly mix again to combine.

Take the soft cheese and drain off any excess water – I find it best to add the cheese to a bowl first, just to make sure. Add the soft cheese to the butter mixture and beat well. At first, it may look a little weird, but continue to beat until the lumps disappear and the frosting is smooth and thick. Slather the spiced soft cheese frosting over the top of the cake and decorate with the reserved toasted nuts.

CHOCOLATE GANACHE DRIP CAKE

There is something about using a smooth and silky ganache to decorate a cake that creates a wonderful flavour, which is luxuriously chocolatey and I want to gobble up every single crumb. I used a mix of dark and milk chocolate to give the ganache a balanced flavour, but if you wanted to use all dark chocolate for extra intensity you would need 300g in total. If you wanted to use milk chocolate, you would need 450g in total, and if you wanted to use white chocolate you would need 600g in total. Any combination works well if you're a chocoholic. Also, be sure to have fun with the decoration – I adored adding the golden touches to this cake.

SERVES: 15+
PREP: 30 minutes
BAKE: 50–60 minutes
COOL: 2 hours
DECORATE: 3 hours
LASTS: 2–3+ days,
in the fridge

500g unsalted butter, at room temperature, plus extra for greasing
500g soft light brown sugar
425g self-raising flour
75g cocoa powder
8–10 eggs
1 tsp vanilla extract

Buttercream

200g unsalted butter, at room temperature
350g icing sugar
50g cocoa powder
2–3 tbsp double cream

see next page

Preheat the oven to 170°C/150°C fan and grease and line two 20cm springform cake tins with parchment paper.

In a large bowl, cream the butter and sugar together until light and fluffy. Add the flour, cocoa powder, eggs and vanilla extract and beat again until well combined.

Divide the mixture between the two tins and bake in the oven for 50–60 minutes, or until a cocktail stick or skewer inserted into the middle of the cakes comes out clean. Leave to cool in the tins for 10 minutes, then turn out onto a wire rack and leave to cool fully.

Buttercream

In a large bowl, beat the butter to loosen it. Add the icing sugar and cocoa powder and beat well until smooth and fluffy. Gradually pour in the double cream, beating continuously until smooth.

Split the two cakes into four layers by slicing each cake in half horizontally, using a long serrated knife.

Put the first cake layer onto a cake board or a flat plate. Using a palette knife, add two tablespoons of buttercream and spread over the top of the layer. Stack and repeat with the second and third sponge layers. Add the final sponge layer on top.

Using the remaining buttercream, spread and smooth a thin layer around the cake sides and top for a crumb coat and chill in the fridge for at least 30 minutes.

Ganache

200g dark chocolate

150g milk chocolate

300ml double cream

Ganache Drip/Decoration

75g dark chocolate

75g milk chocolate

150ml double cream

Sprinkles

Truffles

Ganache

Break the dark chocolate and milk chocolate into equal pieces and put in a heatproof bowl. Heat the double cream in a small pan until just before boiling point. Pour the hot cream over the chocolate and leave to sit for at least 5 minutes. Stir to combine until smooth. If lumps of chocolate still remain, put the mixture back into the pan over a low heat and stir until smooth, or microwave briefly.

Let the ganache cool slightly in the bowl, stirring every few minutes until it forms a peanut-butter-like consistency. The cooling process can be sped up by placing the bowl in the fridge, but be sure to stir it frequently, so it doesn't set too quickly. Once the ganache has set slightly, it can also be whisked with a hand-held electric whisk to give it a lighter and more mousse-like texture.

Remove the chilled cake from the fridge and use a small angled spatula to smooth the ganache over the top and sides of the cake. I use a large metal scraper to achieve an even finish.

Return the cake to chill in the fridge again for at least 30 minutes.

Ganache Drip/Decoration

Break the dark and milk chocolate into equal pieces and add to a heatproof bowl with the double cream. Microwave in short bursts until smooth.

Transfer the mix to a small piping bag or use a teaspoon to drip the ganache down the sides of the cake. The more ganache you push over the edge, the further the drip will fall.

Return the cake to chill in the fridge again for 30 minutes.

Finally, decorate the cake by piping over any leftover ganache or buttercream in swirls, scattering over sprinkles and adding truffles.

RAINBOW PIÑATA CAKE

Say hello to the ultimate birthday celebration cake... this INSANE Rainbow Piñata Cake!
I wanted to create a recipe that is the dream birthday cake and here it is. The rainbow colours
in the sponges, the exploding sweets in the middle, the pink buttercream frosting with
sprinkles studded around... SO MUCH FUN and just as amazing to serve at any celebration.
Jazz it up even further and stuff the cake with sweets and sprinkles of your choice.
Or keep it simple and make it a rainbow cake without the piñata. However you
decorate it, this cake is definitely a showstopper.

SERVES: 15+
PREP: 30 minutes
BAKE: 1 hour
COOL: 2 hours
DECORATE: 2–3 hours
LASTS: 2–3+ days,
in the fridge

600g unsalted butter, at room
    temperature, plus extra for
    greasing
600g caster sugar
600g eggs (10–11 eggs)
600g self-raising flour
2 tsp vanilla extract
½ tsp red, orange, yellow, green,
    blue and purple food colourings

Buttercream

750g unsalted butter, at room
    temperature
1.5kg icing sugar
1 tsp vanilla extract
Food colouring (I used pink)

see next page

Preheat the oven to 160°C/140°C fan and grease and line three
20cm springform cake tins with parchment paper.

In a large bowl, cream 300g of the butter and 300g of the sugar
together until light and fluffy. Add 300g of the eggs, and 300g of
the flour with 1 teaspoon of the vanilla extract and beat again until
smooth.

Divide the mixture evenly between three bowls. Add ½ teaspoon of
red food colouring to one bowl, ½ teaspoon orange food colouring
to another bowl and ½ teaspoon of yellow food colouring to the final
bowl. Transfer each of the coloured mixtures to the three prepared
tins and bake in the oven for 30 minutes, or until a cocktail stick or a
skewer inserted in the middle of the cakes comes out clean.

Leave the cakes to cool in the tins for 10 minutes before turning out
onto a wire rack to cool fully.

Repeat the entire process again, using the remaining green, blue
and purple food colourings to produce three more colourful cakes.

Buttercream

In a large bowl, beat the butter until it is smooth and loose. Add the
icing sugar one-third at a time, beating between additions until fully
combined. Add the vanilla extract and your chosen food colouring
and continue beating the buttercream for 5–6 minutes until fluffy
and light. If the mixture looks too thick, add 1 tablespoon of boiling
water at a time until smooth.

400g chocolate sweets
Leftover buttercream
150g white chocolate
50ml double cream
½ tsp pink food colouring
Sweets
Sprinkles

Lay out the six different-coloured cakes, and in the purple, blue, green, yellow and orange layers, cut a hole in the middle of each cake using a 6–7cm circular cutter. Leave the red sponge whole.

Take the purple cake layer, spread 1–2 tablespoons of the buttercream over the top of the sponge surface avoiding getting any buttercream inside the hole. Stack the blue layer on top of the purple layer and repeat with the green, yellow and orange layers, continuing until all five layers with the hole cut in the centre have been used.

Decoration

Fill the middle cavity with the chocolate sweets. Add the red cake layer on top so the sweets are covered and sealed in.

Spread the buttercream around the edges and sides so the entire cake is covered.

Chill the cake in the fridge for 30 minutes or so to firm up.

Add the white chocolate to a heatproof bowl, and pour on the double cream. Microwave in short bursts, stirring often, until smooth. Once smooth, add the pink food colouring and stir. Add the pink ganache to a small piping bag, or use a teaspoon to drip the ganache down the sides of the cake. Fill in the top with the rest of the ganache, and set the cake in the fridge again for a further 30 minutes.

Remove the cake from the fridge and transfer any leftover buttercream to a piping bag with a piping nozzle of your choice fitted. Pipe the buttercream over the top of the cake and add extra sweets and sprinkles to decorate.

FUNFETTI CAKE

When I see a cake like this, all I can think of is birthdays and parties. Funfetti, if you don't already know, is basically vanilla and sprinkles combined. I love making a cake like this because it always looks so fun and kids go mad for it (although I made one of these for my adult friend's birthday and even she adored it!). Super-bright sprinkles give the best results – the standard supermarket brands can seem a little dull after baking, so try and source good-quality sprinkles if you can. Just look at this cake! It is delicious, super-easy to make and you could go wild with the decoration depending on the theme of your celebration.

SERVES: 12+
PREP: 30 minutes
BAKE: 30–35 minutes
COOL: 2 hours
DECORATE: 1 hour
LASTS: 2–3+ days,
in the fridge

400g unsalted butter, at room
    temperature
400g caster sugar
400g self-raising flour
8 eggs
1 tsp vanilla extract
100–120g funfetti sprinkles
    (supermarket sprinkles won't
    hold their colour as well when
    baked, I use good-quality
    sprinkles from specialist cake
    decorating suppliers)

Buttercream / Decoration

300g unsalted butter, at room
    temperature
600g icing sugar
1 tsp vanilla extract
Funfetti sprinkles

Preheat the oven to 180°C/160°C fan and line three 20cm springform cake tins with parchment paper.

In a large bowl, cream the butter and sugar together until light and fluffy. Add the flour, eggs and vanilla extract to the mix, and beat again until smooth.

Add the funfetti sprinkles and fold through with a spatula. Divide the mixture evenly between the three tins and bake in the oven for 30–35 minutes, or until a cocktail stick or skewer inserted into the middle of the cakes comes out clean.

Leave to cool in the tins for 10–15 minutes, then turn out onto a wire rack to cool fully.

Buttercream / Decoration

In a large bowl, beat the butter for a couple of minutes to loosen it and make it lighter. Add the icing sugar a little at a time and mix well to combine. Add the vanilla extract and beat again. If the mixture feels really stiff, add 1–2 tablespoons of boiling water.

Transfer the mixture to a piping bag with a jumbo round piping tip fitted. Pipe buttercream onto one of the sponge layers, stack the second sponge layer on top and repeat. Finally, add the third sponge layer and pipe over the remaining buttercream. Scatter funfetti sprinkles over the cake and enjoy!

EASTER DRIP CAKE

When I think of Easter I think of chocolate, pastel colours and all things sweet and this cake is the perfect way to celebrate. The theming of the cake works so well because the beautiful colours of the buttercream perfectly complement the Easter eggs and the chocolate cake, but you could bake this at any other time of year too. Think red, white and green for Christmas or purple, green and orange for Halloween. The chocolate drip, the chocolate sponge and the overload of decadence makes for an extraordinary celebration cake. This one always goes down so well... give it a go!

SERVES: 15+
PREP: 30 minutes
BAKE: 30–35 minutes
COOL: 2 hours
DECORATE: 1 hour
LASTS: 2–3+ days,
in the fridge

400g unsalted butter, at room
  temperature
400g soft light brown sugar
350g self-raising flour
75g cocoa powder
8 eggs
1 tsp vanilla extract

Buttercream

500g unsalted butter, at room
  temperature
1kg icing sugar
1 tsp vanilla extract
Purple food colouring
Pink food colouring
White food colouring

Ganache / Decoration

75g milk chocolate
75g dark chocolate
150ml double cream
200g sugar-coated chocolate mini
  eggs (I use Cadbury Mini Eggs)

Preheat the oven to 180°C/160°C fan and line three 20cm springform cake tins with parchment paper.

In a large bowl, cream the butter and sugar together until light and fluffy. Add the flour, cocoa powder, eggs and vanilla extract and beat until smooth.

Divide the mixture evenly between the three tins and bake for 30 minutes – check after 25 minutes, but depending on your oven temperature, baking can take up to 35 minutes. The cakes are ready when a cocktail stick or skewer inserted into the middle comes out clean.

Leave to cool in the tins for 10 minutes, then turn out onto a wire rack to cool fully.

Buttercream

In a large bowl, beat the butter for several minutes until it is really smooth and supple. Add the icing sugar a little at a time, beating after each addition to fully combine. Add the vanilla extract and beat again. If the mixture feels really stiff, add 1–2 tablespoons of boiling water.

Reserve 200g of buttercream for a crumb coat. Divide the remaining buttercream between three bowls (about 430g in each). Colour one batch a light purple, one batch a light pink and the last batch white.

Secure the first cake layer onto a cake board or flat plate, using a little of the buttercream to help it stick. Spread over a couple of tablespoons of purple buttercream, smoothing evenly. Add the

second cake layer and repeat with the pink buttercream.
Add the third and final cake layer. Using the reserved crumb coat buttercream, lightly smooth a thin coating around the edges with a small offset spatula and a cake scraper to seal any gaps and to trap crumbs so that your final icing is crumb-free. Chill in the fridge until firm for about 30 minutes.

Transfer the purple buttercream to a large piping bag, cut the end off, and pipe swirls of purple buttercream around the outside of the first layer. Pipe pink buttercream swirls around the second layer and finally, pipe white swirls around and on top of the third layer. Add more buttercream than you think you need to each layer, as at the next stage some will be removed.

Using a cake scraper, smooth the cake around the sides to create a flat and smooth ombre buttercream. Once smooth and the different colours look as if they are gradually blending into one another, chill in the fridge for about 30 minutes until firm.

Ganache / Decoration

Add the milk and dark chocolate to a heatproof jug or bowl and pour over the double cream. Heat for 30 seconds in the microwave and stir well. Continue to heat in 10-second bursts, stirring every time until the ganache is smooth. Alternatively, set the bowl over a pan of simmering water (bain-marie) to melt the chocolate and cream mixture.

Transfer the ganache to a small piping bag and remove the chilled cake from the fridge. Cut a small amount of the piping bag off, and pipe drips of ganache down the side of the cake, then fill in the top of the cake with ganache and spread it over evenly with a palette knife. Chill in the fridge for about 30 minutes.

Pipe any remaining buttercream over the top of the chilled cake (I used my 2D closed star piping nozzle), and then decorate with chocolate mini eggs! I used whole mini eggs for decorating the top of the buttercream, then filled in the middle with some whole and some chopped mini eggs.

PUMPKIN BUNDT CAKE

When autumn starts and it gets closer to Halloween, I can't help but think of everything and anything to do with pumpkins... so why not make a Pumpkin Bundt Cake? I used tinned pumpkin purée for ease, but if it's near Halloween and you intend to carve your own pumpkin, scoop out the flesh (remove the seeds) and blend to create your own purée. I love the warming spices in this cake, but you can easily adapt them to whatever you prefer or have available – all ground ginger, or all cinnamon... the choice is yours!

SERVES: 15+
PREP: 30 minutes
BAKE: 1+ hours
COOL: 2 hours
DECORATE: 15 minutes
LASTS: 2–3+ days,
in the fridge

275ml sunflower oil/vegetable oil

300g soft light brown sugar

4 eggs

275g tinned pumpkin purée

250g self-raising flour

2 tsp ground cinnamon

½ tsp ground ginger

½ tsp ground nutmeg

¼ tsp allspice

¼ tsp ground cloves

Decoration

150g icing sugar

½ tsp ground cinnamon

1–3 tbsp water

Preheat the oven to 180°C/160°C fan and grease a 10-cup (2½-litre capacity) bundt tin with 2 teaspoons of oil and 2 teaspoons of flour mixed to a paste and brushed all over the inside of the tin.

In a large bowl, add the oil, sugar and eggs and whisk to combine. Add the pumpkin purée and stir again. Finally, add the flour, cinnamon, ginger, nutmeg, allspice and cloves and carefully stir until well combined.

Transfer the mixture to the tin and bake for 1 hour, but it may take a little longer depending on your oven temperature. When ready, the cake should come away from the edges of the tin and a cocktail stick or skewer inserted into the middle will come out clean.

Leave the cake to cool in the tin for at least 20 minutes, before carefully turning out onto a wire rack to cool fully.

Decoration

In a large bowl, add the icing sugar and cinnamon and briefly mix to combine. Add the water 1 tablespoon at a time, mixing well until a thick liquid icing is formed. Transfer the cake to a serving plate and drizzle the icing over the cake.

CHOCOLATE ORANGE YULE LOG

If you have followed my blog for a while, you will know how obsessed I am with all things chocolate orange – it is one of my favourite flavour combinations in the world! When it's the festive season, it's even more of a reason to devour all things chocolate orange, and if you are making this beautiful Chocolate Orange Yule Log Cake you are onto a winner. With a chocolate orange buttercream centre, a luxurious chocolate coating and even more heavenly bits and bobs to sprinkle on top, one slice won't be enough. You can of course switch the orange flavouring to peppermint, or even coffee extract would taste delightful.

SERVES: 15+
PREP: 30 minutes
BAKE: 10 minutes
COOL: 2 hours
DECORATE: 2–3 hours
LASTS: 2–3+ days,
in the fridge

5 eggs
100g caster sugar
75g self-raising flour
45g cocoa powder
Zest of 1 orange or 1 tsp orange
  extract

Buttercream

125g unsalted butter, at room
  temperature, plus extra for
  greasing
225g icing sugar, plus extra
  for dusting
25g cocoa powder
50ml double cream
½ tsp orange extract

see next page

Preheat the oven to 200°C/180°C fan and grease and line a Swiss roll tin (32 x 22cm) with parchment paper.

In a large bowl, whisk the eggs and sugar for about 5 minutes until the mixture is pale and mousse-like in texture.

Sift the flour and cocoa powder into the bowl and add the orange zest or extract. Carefully fold the ingredients together in the bowl until the mixture is combined.

Transfer the mixture to the Swiss roll tin and smooth over evenly. Bake in the oven for 10 minutes.

Take another piece of parchment paper slightly larger than the cake, and dust with icing sugar. Flip the cake onto the sugar-covered piece of parchment paper and carefully remove the original piece of baking parchment from the base of the cake.

While the cake is still warm, roll the sponge and paper together from short side to short side quite tightly and once rolled, leave to cool fully.

Buttercream

In a large bowl, beat the butter for a few minutes to loosen it. Add the icing sugar and cocoa powder and beat again until quite thick. Add the double cream and orange extract, and beat until smooth and well combined. Put to one side.

Ganache

100g dark chocolate
100g milk chocolate
200ml double cream
½ tsp orange extract

Decoration

Icing sugar, for dusting
Chocolate orange slices (I use
  Terry's), crushed
Orange zest
Orange sprinkles

Ganache

Break the dark chocolate and milk chocolate into equal pieces and put in a heatproof bowl. Heat the double cream in a small pan until just before boiling point. Pour the hot cream over the chocolate and leave to sit for at least 5 minutes. Stir to combine until smooth. If lumps of chocolate still remain, put the mixture back into the pan over a low heat and stir until smooth, or microwave briefly.

Chill the ganache mixture in the fridge for 30–45 minutes, and then whisk by hand or with a hand-held electric whisk until smooth and fluffy. Sometimes this can take longer than you might think to get to a whip-able stage.

Decoration

Carefully unroll the cake, trying to avoid breaking the sponge. Don't worry too much if it does though as you can stick it back together.

Spread the buttercream evenly onto the unrolled sponge, and re-roll into the classic Swiss roll shape. Slather the ganache over the outside of the cake with a palette knife and use a fork or a cake skewer lightly dragged through the ganache to create a bark-like effect.

Lightly dust with icing sugar, and sprinkle with crushed chocolate orange slices, some orange zest, or maybe even some orange sprinkles.

PROSECCO CAKE

It's Valentine's Day, the day of romance, and you want to bake a cake that is a little bit special... look no further than this Prosecco Cake! It is indulgent, but not too big. Prosecco-soaked strawberries, a prosecco drizzle, prosecco buttercream... it's the cake of love. Of course, it would make a great cake for other celebrations throughout the year too, such as New Year's Eve or a birthday. Swap the prosecco for champagne or use raspberries instead of strawberries. Try making a chocolate sponge for extra decadence, by substituting 50g of the flour for cocoa powder.

SERVES: 15+
PREP: 1 hour
BAKE: 35–40 minutes
COOL: 2 hours
DECORATE: 1 hour
LASTS: 2–3+ days,
in the fridge

Prep

12 medium fresh strawberries
250ml prosecco

Cake

300g unsalted butter, at room
   temperature, plus extra for
   greasing
300g caster sugar
300g self-raising flour
6 eggs
1 tsp vanilla extract

Drizzle

200ml prosecco (above)
150g caster sugar

see next page

Put the strawberries in a bowl and pour over the prosecco. Leave the strawberries overnight to soak if you have time, reserving the prosecco liquid for later in the recipe.

Cake

Preheat the oven to 180°C/160°C fan and grease and line two 20cm springform cake tins with parchment paper.

In a large bowl, cream the butter and sugar together for 3–4 minutes until light and fluffy. Add the flour, eggs and vanilla extract and beat again for a couple of minutes until smooth.

Divide the mixture evenly between the two tins and bake in the oven for 35–40 minutes, or until a cocktail stick or skewer inserted into the middle of the cakes comes out clean.

Drizzle

Pour the reserved prosecco liquid (that you soaked the strawberries in) into a small pan and add the sugar. Heat over a low heat, stirring continually until the sugar has dissolved.

Gently pour the syrup over the cakes while they are still hot in their tins (reserving a few tablespoons of syrup for later).

Leave the cakes to cool fully in the tins.

Buttercream / Decoration

200g unsalted butter, at room
  temperature
400g icing sugar
3 tbsp prosecco (see page 75)
150g prosecco strawberry jam
  (or plain strawberry jam)
Sprinkles

Buttercream / Decoration

In a large bowl, beat the butter for 3–4 minutes until smooth
and supple. Add the sugar, one half at a time, beating well after
each addition.

Add the reserved prosecco syrup to the buttercream mixture
1 tablespoon at a time, beating well after each addition.

Remove the fully cooled cakes from their tins. Put one sponge layer
onto a flat plate or cake stand and carefully spread the jam over
the top. Transfer the buttercream to a piping bag with a piping
nozzle fitted and pipe half of the prosecco buttercream over the
jam layer. Lay the second sponge layer on top.

Top the cake with buttercream, the reserved prosecco-soaked
strawberries and some sprinkles.

BIRTHDAY CAKE TRAYBAKE

I love a layer cake, I love a drip cake, I love any cake... but sometimes, I want to make something super easy and crowd-pleasing and this Birthday Cake Traybake is a winner every time. Shop-bought traybake cakes can be delicious, but when you can make them so easily yourself and customise the colours or flavours as you please, there's really no comparison. I made a vanilla buttercream frosting and vanilla sponge and then topped it with sprinkles and sweets. However, feel free to get creative and decorate with different sweets, colours or sprinkles to make it Easter-, Christmas- or even Halloween-themed!

SERVES: 18+
PREP: 20 minutes
BAKE: 45–50 minutes
COOL: 2 hours
DECORATE: 20 minutes
LASTS: 2–3+ days,
in the fridge

400g unsalted butter, at room
  temperature, plus extra for
  greasing
400g caster sugar
400g self-raising flour
7–8 eggs
1 tsp vanilla extract

Buttercream

250g unsalted butter, at room
  temperature
500g icing sugar
1 tsp vanilla extract
1 tsp blue food colouring, or any
  colour you want! (optional)

Decoration

Sprinkles
Sweets

Preheat the oven to 180°C/160°C fan and grease and line a 22 x 33cm traybake tin with parchment paper.

In a large bowl, beat together the butter and sugar until light and fluffy. Add the flour, eggs and vanilla extract and beat again until smooth.

Transfer the mixture to the tin and bake in the oven for 45–50 minutes, or until a cocktail stick or skewer inserted into the middle of the cake comes out clean.

Let the cake cool fully in the tin.

Buttercream

In a large bowl, beat the butter for a few minutes to loosen it. Add the icing sugar and beat again until smooth. Add the vanilla extract and food colouring, if using, and beat until well combined.

Decoration

Spread the buttercream over the top of the cake with a palette knife and scatter over sprinkles and sweets for decoration.

Cupcakes and Muffins

MARGARITA CUPCAKES

So, I will say from the beginning that this cupcake recipe is divine and the PERFECT bake for any party... but in my opinion, you can't beat serving them in the summertime. A classic margarita often includes tequila, orange and lime – what forms the lime and orange come in can vary – but for these cupcakes I focused on the tequila and lime only. I wanted a deliciously strong flavour of tequila to soak into the cupcake and be a part of the frosting. However, I also wanted the sweet but slightly sour taste from the lime to come through to keep things fresh. If you do want to add some orange flavour, try adding ½ teaspoon of orange extract to both the cupcake mixture and the buttercream – it is yummy!

MAKES: 12
PREP: 30 minutes
BAKE: 20–22 minutes
COOL: 1 hour
DECORATE: 30 minutes
LASTS: 3+ days, at room temperature

125g unsalted butter or baking spread, at room temperature
200g caster sugar
200g self-raising flour
½ tsp salt
3 eggs
1 tsp vanilla extract
125ml full-fat milk
Zest of 3 limes
180ml tequila

Buttercream

200g unsalted butter, at room temperature
400g icing sugar
50ml tequila
Zest of 1 lime

Decoration

Lime slices
Lime zest
Mini umbrellas

Preheat the oven to 180°C/160°C fan and get 12 cupcake cases ready.

In a large bowl, cream the butter and sugar together until light and fluffy. Add the flour, salt, eggs and vanilla extract and beat to combine. Finally, add the milk and lime zest and beat again.

Divide the mixture equally between the 12 cupcake cases. Transfer to the oven and bake for 20–22 minutes. While still warm, pour 1 tablespoon of tequila over each cupcake. Leave to cool fully on a wire rack.

Buttercream

In a large bowl, beat the butter for a few minutes to loosen it. Gradually beat in the icing sugar until well combined. Pour in the tequila slowly while continuously mixing, add the lime zest and beat the buttercream for a few minutes until light and fluffy.

Decoration

Transfer the buttercream to a piping bag with the piping nozzle of your choice fitted. Pipe the buttercream over the cupcakes however you like.

Top each cupcake with a slice of lime, a sprinkling of lime zest and a mini umbrella.

CHOCOLATE ORANGE CUPCAKES

As you may know already, I am obsessed with this recipe – it was without a doubt one of my blog favourites. I wanted these cupcakes to feature in the book because it is a recipe I make every Christmas without fail. To make a chocolate orange frosting, feel free to add 35g cocoa powder to the buttercream mixture, or even 175g melted milk chocolate.

MAKES: 12
PREP: 30 minutes
BAKE: 18–22 minutes
COOL: 1 hour
DECORATE: 30 minutes
LASTS: 3+ days,
at room temperature

150g unsalted butter or baking
   spread, at room temperature
150g soft light brown sugar
120g self-raising flour
30g cocoa powder
3 eggs
Zest of 1 orange or 1 tsp orange
   extract
150g chocolate orange slices
   (I use Terry's), chopped

Buttercream

150g unsalted butter, at room
   temperature
300g icing sugar
1 tsp orange extract
Orange food colouring

Decoration

50g milk chocolate, melted
   (optional)
Chocolate orange slices
Sprinkles

Preheat the oven to 180°C/160°C fan and get 12 cupcake cases ready.

In a large bowl, cream the butter and sugar together until light and fluffy. Add the flour, cocoa powder, eggs and orange zest or extract to the bowl and beat until the mixture is smooth. Fold through the chopped chocolate orange slices.

Divide the mixture evenly between the 12 cupcake cases. Transfer the cupcakes to the oven and bake for 18–22 minutes. Leave to cool fully on a wire rack.

Buttercream

In a large bowl, beat the butter for a few minutes to loosen it. Add the icing sugar and beat again until well combined. Add the orange extract and orange food colouring and beat again. The amount of food colouring needed depends on the brand used – add a little at a time to achieve your desired colour.

Decoration

Transfer the buttercream to a piping bag with a piping nozzle fitted and pipe over the cupcakes.

Carefully drizzle the melted chocolate over the cupcakes, if you like. Add a chocolate orange slice to each cupcake and scatter over some sprinkles.

RAINBOW CUPCAKES

We all love an explosion of colour, and these rainbow cupcakes do just that. Red, orange, yellow, green, blue and purple all dolloped together into a cupcake, topped with a delicious soft cheese frosting. I flavoured my cupcakes with vanilla because we all know how much I love vanilla, but you could spice these up a bit and use any other flavours – lemon, orange, or even almond. The soft cheese frosting cuts through the sweetness of the cupcakes and balances them perfectly. If you prefer, you could use two colours, or even three or four – just be sure to split the mixture evenly and have fun!

MAKES: 12
PREP: 45 minutes
BAKE: 20–22 minutes
COOL: 1 hour
DECORATE: 30 minutes
LASTS: 3+ days,
at room temperature

200g unsalted butter or baking
    spread, at room temperature
200g caster sugar
200g self-raising flour
4 eggs
1 tsp vanilla extract
¼ tsp red, orange, yellow, green,
    blue and purple food colouring

Buttercream
150g unsalted butter, at room
    temperature
150g icing sugar
300g full-fat soft cheese
½ tsp vanilla extract

Decoration
Rainbow sprinkles

Preheat the oven to 180°C/160°C fan and get 12 cupcake cases ready.

In a large bowl, cream the butter and sugar together until light and fluffy. Add the flour, eggs and vanilla extract to the bowl and beat until the mixture is smooth. Divide the mixture equally between six small bowls. Colour each bowl with a different one of the six food colourings.

Carefully distribute each colour between the 12 cupcake cases using teaspoons – either randomly, or layering consecutive colours in the cupcake cases to form a rainbow-like pattern. Be careful not to mix the different-colour mixtures together otherwise your cupcake colours will lose their clarity.

Transfer the cupcakes to the oven and bake for 20–22 minutes. Leave to cool fully on a wire rack.

Buttercream

In a large bowl, beat the butter for a few minutes to loosen it. Gradually beat in the icing sugar until well combined. Take the soft cheese and drain off any excess water – I find it best to add the soft cheese to a bowl first, just to make sure. Beat the soft cheese into the butter and icing sugar mixture until all lumps disappear and the mixture is smooth. Finally, add the vanilla extract and beat to combine.

Decoration

Transfer the buttercream to a piping bag with the piping nozzle of your choice fitted. Pipe the buttercream over the cupcakes however you like. Sprinkle some rainbow sprinkles over each cupcake.

LOVE HEART CUPCAKES

Please can we take a moment to revel in how cute these cupcakes are, with little baby hearts hidden inside every single one? I know I have already mentioned in this book how you probably want dessert for Valentine's Day to be quick and easy, but these are the bake to make if you want to go that extra mile and seriously impress. I used a vanilla cupcake, but you can make these chocolate by substituting 25g of flour for cocoa powder in the main cupcake mix. The swirl of pink buttercream frosting on top finishes off these beautiful cupcakes, which are the perfect gift for your loved ones.

MAKES: 12
PREP: 1 hour
BAKE: 35–45 minutes
COOL: 3 hours
DECORATE: 30 minutes
LASTS: 3+ days,
at room temperature

Red Cupcake Hearts

100g unsalted butter or baking
  spread, at room temperature
100g caster sugar
100g self-raising flour
2 eggs
1 tsp red food colouring

Cupcakes

150g unsalted butter or baking
  spread, at room temperature
150g caster sugar
150g self-raising flour
3 eggs
1 tsp vanilla extract

see next page

Red Cupcake Hearts

Preheat the oven to 180°C/160°C fan and grease and line a 20cm square tin with parchment paper.

In a large bowl, cream the butter and sugar together until light and fluffy. Add the flour, eggs and red food colouring to the bowl and beat again until smooth and even in colour.

Pour the mixture into the cake tin and bake for 20–22 minutes. Leave to cool for 10 minutes in the tin and then turn out onto a wire rack to cool fully.

Using a small 3cm heart-shaped cutter, cut small shapes out of the cooled red sponge and reserve for later.

Cupcakes

For the cupcakes, leave the oven preheated to 180°C/160°C fan and get 12 cupcake cases ready.

In a large bowl, cream the butter and sugar together until light and fluffy. Add the flour, eggs and vanilla extract and beat until the mixture is smooth.

Add a tablespoon of mixture to each cupcake case. Add an upright red sponge heart to each cupcake, carefully pushing it down so that it sits in the cupcake mixture. Top each cupcake with another tablespoon of mixture, sharing among the cupcake cases evenly until the mixture is used up.

Buttercream

200g unsalted butter, at room
   temperature
425g icing sugar
1 tsp vanilla extract
1 tsp pink food colouring

Decoration

Sprinkles

Transfer the cupcakes to the oven and bake for 18–22 minutes. Leave to cool fully on a wire rack.

Buttercream

In a large bowl, beat the butter for a few minutes to loosen it. Gradually beat in the icing sugar until well combined. Add the vanilla extract and pink food colouring and beat for a few minutes until light and fluffy. If the mixture is thick, add 1–2 tablespoons of boiling water to loosen it slightly, but this is not essential.

Decoration

Transfer the buttercream to a piping bag with the piping nozzle of your choice fitted. Pipe the buttercream over the cupcakes however you like and scatter over some sprinkles.

GHOST CUPCAKES

I know Halloween is meant to be scary or spooky, but these cupcakes are anything but frightening. I can't even cope. A yummy and easy chocolate cupcake topped with an Italian meringue ghost – spook-scrumptious! (Maybe not the best marriage of words but, they are delicious.) An Italian meringue can sound a little complicated, but it is always worth it. You can flavour the Italian meringue to jazz up the cupcakes, or even core out some of the middle of each and add 1 teaspoon of chocolate spread per cupcake before adding the meringue topping.

MAKES: 12
PREP: 45 minutes
BAKE: 18–22 minutes
COOL: 1 hour
DECORATE: 30 minutes
LASTS: 2+ days,
in the fridge

150g unsalted butter or baking
   spread, at room temperature
150g soft light brown sugar
125g self-raising flour
25g cocoa powder
3 eggs

Meringue Topping
185g granulated sugar
85ml water
100g egg whites
20g dark chocolate, melted
   or chocolate sprinkles

Preheat the oven to 180°C/160°C fan and get 12 cupcake cases ready.

In a large bowl, cream the butter and sugar together until light and fluffy. Add the flour, cocoa powder and eggs to the bowl and beat until the mixture is smooth. Divide the mixture evenly between the 12 cupcakes cases. Transfer the cupcakes to the oven and bake for 18–22 minutes. Leave to cool fully on a wire rack.

Meringue Topping

Put the sugar and the water into a heavy-based pan and bring to the boil, stirring occasionally with a wooden spoon. When the mixture starts to boil, monitor the temperature with a sugar thermometer until it reaches 120°C (firm ball stage) . If any sugar splashes up the sides of the pan while boiling, brush the insides of the pan with a pastry brush dipped in cold water. This will stop the mixture from crystallising.

Using a clean bowl and whisk (otherwise the egg whites won't stiffen), add the egg whites to the bowl and whisk until stiff peaks form. Start to pour the hot sugar syrup onto the stiffened egg whites at the edge of the bowl while continuously whisking – make sure you do this slowly so it is a constant trickle of sugar syrup and the egg whites stay smooth. Once all of the sugar syrup has been incorporated, continue to whisk for 5–7 minutes until the mixture is smooth and has cooled down.

Transfer the meringue to a piping bag fitted with a large round nozzle. Pipe the meringue onto each cupcake, pointing the nozzle downwards to create a wider bottom, then lift slightly as you release. Repeat with a slightly smaller blob and lift for a smaller top.

Pipe eyes and a mouth with the melted dark chocolate, or use sprinkles instead.

CHOCOLATE EGG CUPCAKES

Can we appreciate that a cupcake stuffed with a soft-centred Easter chocolate is something that is quite hard to beat? Add to that a silky-smooth buttercream frosting and even more Easter chocolate goodness to decorate and you're onto a winner! Swap the mini filled chocolate eggs for other chocolates of your choice – caramel-centred chocolates would work well. These cupcakes are one of the best ways to celebrate Easter. Get together with your loved ones and double the quantity of the recipe as I promise you everyone will want a second!

MAKES: 12
PREP: 2 hours
BAKE: 18–22 minutes
COOL: 1 hour
DECORATE: 30 minutes
LASTS: 3+ days,
at room temperature

12 mini filled chocolate eggs
   (I use mini Crème eggs), frozen
150g unsalted butter or baking
   spread, at room temperature
150g soft light brown sugar
125g self-raising flour
25g cocoa powder
3 eggs

Buttercream

150g unsalted butter, room
   temperature
300g icing sugar
1 tsp vanilla extract
½ tsp yellow food colouring
½ tsp orange food colouring

Decoration

Sprinkles
6 filled chocolate eggs (I use
   Crème eggs), halved

Make sure your mini filled chocolate eggs are frozen.

Preheat the oven to 180°C/160°C fan. Get 12 cupcake cases ready.

In a large bowl, cream the butter and sugar together until light and fluffy. Add the flour, cocoa powder and eggs to the bowl and combine well until the mixture is smooth.

Spoon a tablespoon of cupcake mixture into each cupcake case and put a frozen mini filled chocolate egg on top of each. Spoon over another tablespoon of cupcake mixture in each to cover the chocolate egg. Transfer the cupcakes to the oven and bake for 18–22 minutes. Leave to cool fully on a wire rack.

Buttercream

In a large bowl, beat the butter for a couple of minutes to loosen it. Gradually beat in the icing sugar until well combined, then add the vanilla extract and beat for 5 minutes until the buttercream has a silky texture. If the mixture is a little stiff, add 1 tablespoon of boiling water at a time until you reach the consistency you want!

Divide the mixture into two equal batches. Add both the yellow and orange food colouring to one batch to make a yolk colour and beat until smooth. Leave the other batch as it is.

Decoration

Transfer the two different coloured buttercreams to the same piping bag, one colour on each side of the piping bag so that the colours swirl together when piped. Using a piping nozzle of your choice, pipe the buttercream onto the cupcakes. Scatter over some sprinkles and add half a filled chocolate egg to each cupcake.

EXPLODING CUPCAKES

I always want to bake something fun during bonfire season, because all I can think of is fireworks! The colours, the explosions and all things autumnal – these cupcakes 100% represent that. A delightfully cinnamon-hinted chocolate cupcake stuffed with bright sprinkles for an 'explosion', frosted with scrumptious buttercream and even more exploding fun on top. I love the super-bright purple frosting, but you can use any colour and any sprinkles you like. Go silver and gold for New Year's Eve perhaps? Or even red and pink for Valentine's Day.

MAKES: 12
PREP: 30 minutes
BAKE: 18–22 minutes
COOL: 1 hour
DECORATE: 30 minutes
LASTS: 3+ days,
at room temperature

150g unsalted butter or baking
  spread, at room temperature
150g soft light brown sugar
125g self-raising flour
25g cocoa powder
3 eggs
½ tsp ground cinnamon
100g sprinkles

Buttercream

150g unsalted butter, at room
  temperature
350g icing sugar
½ tsp vanilla extract
Food colouring of your choice
  (I use purple)

Decoration

Sprinkles
Popping candy
Mini sparklers

Preheat the oven to 180°C/160°C fan and get 12 cupcake cases ready.

In a large bowl, cream the butter and sugar together until light and fluffy. Add the flour, cocoa powder, eggs and cinnamon to the bowl and beat until the mixture is smooth.

Divide the mixture equally between the 12 cupcake cases. Transfer the cupcakes to the oven and bake for 18–22 minutes. Leave to cool fully on a wire rack.

Core out the cupcakes and fill each hole with 1–2 teaspoons of sprinkles.

Buttercream

In a large bowl, beat the butter for a few minutes to loosen it. Gradually beat in the icing sugar until well combined, then add the vanilla extract and beat again. Add your chosen food colouring to the mixture and stir well until your desired colour is achieved.

Decoration

Transfer the buttercream to a piping bag with the piping nozzle of your choice fitted and pipe over the cupcakes however you like. Add some more sprinkles and popping candy to the top of each cupcake and serve with a lit mini sparkler stuck in for extra oomph!

GINGERBREAD WHITE CHOCOLATE CUPCAKES

Ginger sponge takes cake to a whole new level. The mixture of golden syrup, ground ginger and dark brown sugar creates a cupcake sponge that is out of this world amazing, if I do say so myself. Stuff these cupcakes with a white chocolate filling and, oh my, ginger and white chocolate combine to create one of the most elite flavour combinations. Make these for any celebration (but obviously Christmas most of all). Why not bake a batch for a little festive gift... to yourself?

MAKES: 12
PREP: 30 minutes
BAKE: 20–22 minutes
COOL: 1 hour
DECORATE: 30 minutes
LASTS: 3+ days,
at room temperature

125g unsalted butter or baking spread, at room temperature
125g soft dark brown sugar
250g golden syrup
250g self-raising flour
2 tsp ground ginger
2 eggs
175ml full-fat milk

Buttercream

200g white chocolate
175g unsalted butter, at room temperature
350g icing sugar
1 tsp ground ginger

Decoration

150g white chocolate spread
50g white chocolate, melted
White chocolate chips
Gingerbread sprinkles/cake toppers

Preheat the oven to 180°C/160°C fan. Get 12 cupcake cases ready.

Put the butter, sugar and golden syrup into a medium pan. Heat over a low-medium heat until the butter has melted and the sugar has dissolved. Leave to cool.

In a large bowl, add the flour and ginger and mix together. Pour in the cooled butter mixture and stir until combined. Add the eggs and milk and briefly stir until just combined. Divide the mixture evenly between the 12 cupcakes cases. Transfer to the oven and bake for 20–22 minutes. Leave to cool fully on a wire rack.

Buttercream

In a small heatproof bowl, break up pieces of the white chocolate and heat in short bursts in the microwave until smooth or set the bowl over a pan of simmering water (bain-marie). Leave to cool for at least 5 minutes.

In a large bowl, beat the butter for a couple of minutes to loosen it. Gradually beat in the icing sugar until well combined. Add the cooled melted white chocolate and the ginger and beat again. If the mixture is extremely thick, add 1–2 tablespoons of boiling water to loosen slightly, but this is not essential.

Decoration

Core out the cupcakes and fill each hole with a spoonful of white chocolate spread. Transfer the buttercream to a piping bag with a piping nozzle of your choice fitted. Pipe the buttercream onto the cupcakes however you like. Drizzle over the melted white chocolate, and decorate with some white chocolate chips and gingerbread sprinkles/cake toppers.

APPLE CRUMBLE MUFFINS

An apple crumble is the most warming dessert, especially when it is colder outside, so turning that wholesome, familiar flavour into a muffin is the dream! These beauties are softly spiced, stuffed with apple chunks and topped with a homemade crumble (you can of course use shop-bought crumble if you're short on time). I drizzle my muffins with a cinnamon-spiced icing, but imagine these served with a splash of custard... HEAVENLY! If you wanted to bake these at a non-autumnal time of year, you could always use other fruit – blackberries or cherries would work well, just keep the weight of the fruit the same.

MAKES: 12
PREP: 30 minutes
BAKE: 22–26 minutes
COOL: 1 hour
DECORATE: 10 minutes
LASTS: 3+ days,
at room temperature

125g unsalted butter or baking
   spread, at room temperature
150g soft light brown sugar
3 eggs
150g soured cream/natural
   yoghurt
1 tsp vanilla extract
250g plain flour
1 tsp baking powder
1 tsp bicarbonate of soda
1 tsp ground cinnamon
½ tsp ground ginger
150g Bramley apples, peeled,
   cored and cut into 1cm chunks

Topping

80g plain flour
40g soft light brown sugar
40g chilled unsalted butter, cubed

Decoration

100g icing sugar
½ tsp ground cinnamon
2–3 tsp water

Preheat the oven to 190°C/170°C fan and get 12 muffin cases ready.

In a large bowl, cream the butter and sugar together until combined. Add the eggs, soured cream or natural yoghurt and the vanilla extract and beat to combine. Add the flour, baking powder, bicarbonate of soda, cinnamon and ginger to the bowl and beat until the mixture is smooth. Fold the apple chunks through the mixture.

Divide the mixture equally between the 12 muffin cases.

Topping

In a large bowl, add the flour, sugar and butter and rub together with your fingertips until the mixture resembles breadcrumbs. Spoon the crumble mixture over the muffins and transfer to the oven to bake for 22–26 minutes. Leave to cool fully on a wire rack.

Decoration

In a bowl, add the icing sugar and cinnamon and mix to combine. Gradually add 1 teaspoon of water at a time, stirring after each addition until the mixture becomes thick, but still runny enough to drip from a spoon. Drizzle the icing over the muffins.

STICKY TOFFEE MUFFINS

One of the most comforting desserts in the world is sticky toffee pudding and I love it in all forms. Something about the mix of dates, golden syrup, sugar and fudge chunks creates an absolute dream combination of flavours. I used fudge chunk 'sprinkles' from the supermarket for these as they form delightful little pockets of gooeyness when baked. You can use chocolate chips, or anything else you fancy instead and making a small amount of toffee sauce for decoration is well worth the effort. Equally, you can leave these plain if you prefer. I just want all the sticky toffee flavour I can get!

MAKES: 12
PREP: 45 minutes
BAKE: 22–24 minutes
COOL: 1 hour
DECORATE: 15 minutes
LASTS: 3+ days, at room temperature

200g medjool dates

1 tsp bicarbonate of soda

150ml boiling water

75g unsalted butter or baking spread, at room temperature

150g soft light brown sugar/soft dark brown sugar

225g self-raising flour

½ tsp vanilla extract

2 eggs

50g golden syrup/black treacle

100g fudge chunk sprinkles

Topping

90g white chocolate

30ml double cream

25g toffee sauce (see page 32)

50g fudge chunk sprinkles

Preheat the oven to 190°C/170°C fan and get 12 muffin cases ready.

Remove any stones from the dates if they have them, and finely chop the dates. Put the chopped dates in a bowl and sprinkle over the bicarbonate of soda. Pour the boiling water over the dates and leave the mixture for 10 minutes.

In a large bowl, cream the butter and light or dark brown sugar together until combined. Add the flour, vanilla extract, eggs and golden syrup or black treacle and beat again until well combined. Add the reserved date mixture and beat again. Finally, fold through the fudge chunk sprinkles.

Divide the mixture equally between the 12 muffin cases. Transfer to the oven to bake for 22–24 minutes. Leave to cool fully on a wire rack.

Topping

In a small heatproof bowl, break up the white chocolate into pieces and pour in the double cream. Melt together in the microwave in short bursts or set the bowl over a pan of simmering water (bain-marie).

Once the mixture is smooth and thick, stir through the toffee sauce. Dollop a spoonful of the mixture on each muffin and sprinkle over some fudge chunks.

S'MORES MUFFINS

A s'more is typically a combination of biscuit, marshmallow and chocolate, so can you imagine anything better than a muffin version? Here I've created a vanilla muffin, studded with chocolate-chip biscuit pieces and topped with marshmallow fluff and a sprinkling of biscuit crumbs. These beauties encapsulate all things autumnal and 'bonfire' and I am here for it. I used dark chocolate chips in my muffins, but you can use milk or even white if you prefer. I kept the digestive biscuits in quite large chunks, but again you can switch for your favourite biscuit and choose your chunk size! Marshmallow fluff is the way to go, as normal marshmallows can dissolve – but if you want, you can add a normal-sized marshmallow on top of each baked muffin and grill it until melted.

MAKES: 12
PREP: 30 minutes
BAKE: 22–25 minutes
COOL: 1 hour
DECORATE: 15 minutes
LASTS: 2+ days,
at room temperature

200g self-raising flour
½ tsp sea salt
125g soft light brown sugar
150ml buttermilk
2 eggs
125ml sunflower oil/vegetable oil
½ tsp vanilla extract
200g dark chocolate chips
150g biscuits, chopped
200g marshmallow fluff

Topping

50g biscuits, crushed to
    fine crumbs
1 tsp soft light brown sugar
15g unsalted butter, melted

Preheat the oven to 190°C/170°C fan and get 12 muffin cases ready.

In a large bowl, add the flour, sea salt and sugar and mix briefly to combine. Add the buttermilk, eggs, oil and vanilla extract and whisk lightly until just combined. Finally, fold through the chocolate chips and chopped biscuits.

Divide the mixture equally between the 12 muffin cases. Dollop a teaspoon of marshmallow fluff onto each muffin.

Topping

In a large bowl, mix the biscuit crumbs, sugar and melted butter together to make a crumble topping. Sprinkle the crumble over the marshmallow fluff and the muffins.

Transfer the muffins to the oven and bake for 22–25 minutes. Leave to cool fully on a wire rack.

Cookies and Biscuits

MELTING MOMENTS

You can argue about the merits of a classic Melting Moment, as they often come in various forms – but for me, it's these deliciously buttery cookies that win, sandwiched together with an unbelievably light and sweet buttercream. These magically melt in the mouth because of the cornflour and icing sugar – both ingredients that give the perfect texture that I love. The dough is easy to roll and I enjoy lightly pressing each cookie down with a fork to get the classic shape. You can then bake, cool and fill, and most importantly, devour every single morsel.

MAKES: 15
PREP: 20 minutes
BAKE: 15 minutes
COOL: 30 minutes
FILL: 30 minutes
LASTS: 3–4+ days, at room temperature

200g unsalted butter, at room temperature
100g icing sugar
1 tsp vanilla extract
235g plain flour
25g cornflour

Filling

100g unsalted butter, at room temperature
200g icing sugar
1 tsp vanilla extract

Preheat the oven to 180°C/160°C fan and line two large baking trays with parchment paper.

In a large bowl, cream the butter and icing sugar together until smooth. Add the vanilla extract, plain flour and cornflour and beat to combine.

Portion the dough out into 30 balls and put them onto the lined baking trays. Squash each cookie ball slightly with a fork to flatten to about half their current height. Bake in the oven for 15 minutes, or until lightly golden. Leave to cool on the trays for 10 minutes, and then transfer to a wire rack to cool fully.

Filling

In a large bowl, beat the butter for 5 minutes until smooth. Add the icing sugar and vanilla extract and beat again for another 5 minutes until light and fluffy. Transfer the filling mixture to a piping bag and with the piping nozzle of your choice fitted, pipe some buttercream onto 15 of the cookies. Sandwich the cookies together with the remaining 15 cookies.

CHOCOLATE HAZELNUT SPREAD STUFFED COOKIES

Imagine one of the most tasty flavours of cookie you've ever come across and then make it even better by stuffing it with a spread. This thick chocolate chip cookie dough with chopped hazelnuts, stuffed with chocolate hazelnut spread is utterly scrumptious. The beauty of this bake is that the cookie dough doesn't need to be chilled, but you do need to make sure that the spread you are using is frozen first, otherwise you will end up in a bit of a cookie mess... trust me, I've been there. If you don't like hazelnuts, leave them out or just replace them with even more chocolate!

MAKES: 12
PREP: 20 minutes
CHILL: 1+ hours
BAKE: 11–13 minutes
COOL: 30 minutes
LASTS: 3–4+ days, at room temperature

12 heaped tsp chocolate hazelnut spread (I use Nutella)

125g unsalted butter, at room temperature

175g soft light brown sugar

1 tsp vanilla extract

1 egg

250g plain flour

35g cocoa powder

½ tsp bicarbonate of soda

½ tsp sea salt

200g milk chocolate chips

100g hazelnuts, chopped

Line a baking tray with parchment paper and scoop 12 heaped teaspoons of chocolate hazelnut spread onto the tray. Transfer to the freezer for at least 1 hour.

Meanwhile, preheat the oven to 190°C/170°C fan. In a large bowl, cream together the butter and sugar until fluffy and light. Add the vanilla extract and egg and beat until smooth.

In a separate bowl, whisk together the flour, cocoa powder, bicarbonate of soda and sea salt, add to the butter/sugar mixture and combine. Add the chocolate chips and chopped hazelnuts and mix until evenly distributed.

Line two baking trays with parchment paper. Portion the dough into 12. Flatten each cookie dough ball slightly in your hand and press a frozen lump of chocolate hazelnut spread into the middle of each cookie. Wrap the cookie dough around the frozen spread, making sure it is sealed. Place the cookies onto the two lined trays.

Bake in the oven for 11–13 minutes. Leave to cool on the trays for 30 minutes before devouring.

SHORTBREAD HEARTS

Shortbread is one of the easiest bakes in the world as it has only three ingredients! This recipe produces sweet, buttery, delicious cookies that you can adapt and change as you please and they are therefore one of the best homemade gifts you can give as their versatility means you can use different shapes to celebrate anything you fancy. I coated my Shortbread Hearts in milk and white chocolate to give them that extra special finishing touch. For an alternative flavour, try adding 1 teaspoon of flavouring extract to the shortbread or add 100–200g chocolate chips.

MAKES: 15
PREP: 15 minutes
CHILL: 30 minutes
BAKE: 15–20 minutes
COOL: 1 hour
DECORATE: 30 minutes
LASTS: 3–4+ days, at room temperature

200g unsalted butter, at room temperature
100g caster sugar, plus extra for sprinkling
300g plain flour, plus extra for dusting

Decoration

125g white chocolate
125g milk chocolate
Sprinkles

Line two baking trays with parchment paper.

In a large bowl, cream the butter and sugar until light and fluffy. Add the flour and beat until a smooth dough is formed.

Turn out onto a lightly floured work surface and roll out the dough until 1cm thick. Using a 7cm heart cutter, cut the cookies out and carefully transfer them to the lined trays using a thin spatula. Chill in the fridge for 30 minutes.

Meanwhile, preheat the oven to 180°C/160°C fan. Sprinkle a little extra caster sugar over the chilled shortbread hearts and bake in the oven for 15–20 minutes, or until light golden in colour. Leave to cool fully on the trays.

Decoration

Melt the white chocolate in one heatproof bowl and the milk chocolate in another heatproof bowl in short bursts in the microwave, or set the bowls over a pan of simmering water (a bain-marie). Dip one half of each shortbread into either the melted white chocolate or milk chocolate.

Once dipped, lay the shortbread hearts back onto the baking trays and drizzle over any leftover chocolate. Scatter over some sprinkles and return them to the fridge to set.

CINNAMON SWIRL COOKIES

I adore anything cinnamon themed, especially cinnamon rolls (can you honestly beat them?). They are one of the most popular recipes on my blog and from my first book, so I thought, why not bake something I know you all want? A cookie version! I made sure to follow the same idea as regular cinnamon bread rolls – bake a 'plain' vanilla dough, spread cinnamon sugar onto the dough and roll up tightly. Drizzle over a sweet sugar icing for extra flavour and enjoy with a steaming cup of coffee on a cold day. These also make great homemade gifts, just pop them in a bag or box with a nice ribbon and they'll go down a treat.

MAKES: 20
PREP: 30 minutes
CHILL: 1+ hours
BAKE: 10–11 minutes
COOL: 30 minutes
DECORATE: 15 minutes
LASTS: 3–4+ days,
at room temperature

300g plain flour, plus extra for
    dusting
¼ tsp salt
½ tsp baking powder
175g unsalted butter, at room
    temperature
150g caster sugar
1 egg
1 tsp vanilla extract

Filling

50g caster sugar
1 tbsp ground cinnamon
15g unsalted butter, melted

Icing

100g icing sugar
2–3 tsp water
½ tsp vanilla extract

In a bowl, add the flour, salt and baking powder and mix to combine.

In a separate large bowl, beat the butter for a minute or two until smooth. Add the sugar and beat again until creamy. Add the egg and vanilla extract and beat until combined. Add the dry ingredients to the wet ingredients and mix until combined. Turn out the dough onto a lightly floured work surface and roll out into a rectangle until it is about ½cm thick.

Filling

In a small bowl, mix together the sugar and cinnamon. Use a pastry brush to brush the melted butter over the top of the dough and then sprinkle over the cinnamon sugar.

Tightly roll the cookie dough into a sausage shape, from one long side to the other long side. Transfer to a tray and chill in the fridge for at least 1 hour.

Meanwhile, preheat the oven to 180°C/160°C fan and line 2–3 large baking trays with parchment paper. Remove the dough from the fridge and slice into 1cm-thick cookies with a sharp knife. Put the cookies onto the trays, allowing space between each cookie for spreading slightly. Bake in the oven for 10–11 minutes until lightly golden. Leave the cookies to cool on the tray for at least 10 minutes, then transfer to wire racks to cool fully.

Icing

In a bowl, whisk the icing sugar, water and vanilla extract together and drizzle over the cookies. Let the icing 'set' for about 30 minutes.

CHOCOLATE COOKIE PIE

A giant Chocolate Cookie Pie with a double chocolate chip cookie dough, a chocolate spread filling and even more chocolate... one for the chocoholics! Cookie pies are one of the most indulgent and delectable bakes that you can make and I can't get enough of them – just look at it. I love this bake because you can swap the flavours of the cookie dough (remove the cocoa powder and add 75g more flour for a plain cookie dough) or even switch the spread you use to a different flavour. This is one of the easiest bakes to customise as the recipe is very forgiving.

SERVES: 15+
PREP: 2 hours
CHILL/SET: 8+ hours
BAKE: 30 minutes
LASTS: 3–4+ days,
at room temperature

200g unsalted butter, at room
  temperature
225g soft light brown sugar
100g white granulated sugar
1 egg
1 egg yolk
1 tsp vanilla extract
350g plain flour
50g cocoa powder
1 tbsp cornflour
1 tsp bicarbonate of soda
½ tsp sea salt
400g milk chocolate chips
750g chocolate hazelnut spread
  (I use Nutella)
200g chocolates

Line the bottom of a 20cm springform cake tin with parchment paper.

In a large bowl, cream the butter, brown sugar and white sugar together until smooth. Add the egg, egg yolk and vanilla extract and beat again. Add the flour, cocoa powder, cornflour, bicarbonate of soda and sea salt and beat until a thick cookie dough is formed.

Add in the chocolate chips and mix until well distributed. Divide the cookie dough into three equal portions – each should weigh about 475g. Press one-third of the cookie dough into the bottom of the lined cake tin. Press another third of the cookie dough around the sides of the cake tin as evenly as possible.

Put the chocolate hazelnut spread in a small heatproof bowl and microwave for 20 seconds to loosen it slightly. Alternatively, mix in a bowl briefly to loosen. Pour into the cookie dough case that you have formed inside the tin. Press the chocolates into the spread.

Transfer the pie to the freezer for 1 hour. Once frozen, remove from the freezer and cover the top of the cookie pie with the final third of cookie dough, sealing it well at the edges. Return the cookie pie to the freezer for another hour while you preheat the oven to 200°C/180°C fan.

Transfer the cookie pie to the oven and bake for 30 minutes until golden on top. Leave to cool in the tin for 1 hour. Return the cookie pie to the fridge and chill for a further 5–6 hours, or preferably overnight. Carefully remove from the tin and use a large, sharp knife to cut the pie into slices.

ETON MESS COOKIES

I have always loved the combination of meringue, fruit and cream and we all know and appreciate my obsession with cookies... so I thought I would combine the two! These quirky Eton Mess Cookies are a delightful mix of ingredients, with two crisp meringue cookies sandwiched around a vanilla buttercream frosting and jam, then perhaps drizzled with white chocolate, if you like. I enjoy these just as they are, but you can definitely switch them up and experiment with different flavours – try dark or milk chocolate drizzled on top, or even a different flavour buttercream in the middle. However you flavour them, these cookies are the ideal way to celebrate summer and are the perfect bake to bring along to a BBQ.

MAKES: 10
PREP: 20 minutes
BAKE: 35–40 minutes
COOL: 30+ minutes
DECORATE: 30 minutes
LASTS: 3–4+ days,
at room temperature

5 egg whites
225g caster sugar
½ tsp vanilla extract

Filling / Decoration

100g unsalted butter, at room
  temperature
200g icing sugar
1 tsp vanilla extract
75g jam
75g white chocolate, melted
  (optional)

Preheat the oven to 120°C/100°C fan and line two large baking trays with parchment paper.

Using a clean bowl and whisk (otherwise the egg whites won't stiffen), add the egg whites to the bowl and whisk until stiff peaks form. Start adding 1 teaspoon of sugar at a time, while continuously whisking. Once all the sugar has been incorporated, add the vanilla extract and whisk for another few minutes.

Carefully transfer the meringue mixture to a piping bag with a star nozzle fitted and pipe 20 swirls about 6–7cm wide on the lined baking trays. Bake in the oven for 35–40 minutes until the meringues are hard on the outside. Leave to cool in the oven with the door shut for 30 minutes, and then remove from the oven and leave to cool fully.

Filling / Decoration

In a large bowl, beat the butter for a few minutes to soften it. Gradually add the icing sugar and vanilla extract and beat the mixture for a few minutes until light and fluffy.

Transfer the buttercream mixture to a piping bag and pipe the buttercream in swirls onto half of the meringue cookies. Spread the jam slightly over the buttercream. Sandwich with another meringue to make a filled meringue cookie.

On a piece of parchment paper (to create less mess), carefully drizzle the melted white chocolate over the meringues for extra pizzazz, if you like.

GINGERBREAD BISCUITS

Gingerbread biscuits are an iconic festive bake that I just can't get enough of at Christmas. The dough for these biscuits is so easy to make and takes barely any time at all – try to work the dough as little as possible so that the biscuits don't become tough. You can shape these using any cutters of your choice – trees, candy canes, snowmen, reindeer or people. Have fun and decorate them as you wish for any celebration!

MAKES: 15
PREP: 30 minutes
BAKE: 10–11 minutes
LASTS: 2+ weeks, at room temperature

375g plain flour

1 tsp bicarbonate of soda

3 tsp ground ginger

120g chilled unsalted butter, cubed

175g soft light brown sugar

100g golden syrup

1 egg

Preheat the oven to 190°C/170°C fan and line three baking trays with parchment paper.

In a large bowl, add the flour, bicarbonate of soda, ginger and butter and rub together with your fingertips until the mixture resembles breadcrumbs. (Alternatively, pulse the ingredients in a food processor.)

Add the sugar to the mix and combine and then add the golden syrup and egg, beating until a smooth dough is formed. Bring the mixture together with your hands, turn out onto a lightly floured work surface and knead for a couple of minutes.

Roll out the dough until ½cm thick and using your chosen cutters, make 15 gingerbread people, snowmen or Christmas trees. Put them onto the lined trays and bake in the oven for 10–11 minutes. Leave to cool fully on a wire rack and either leave plain or decorate how you please.

FIREWORK COOKIES

I adore a sugar cookie because it is so simple and sweet to make, but when you top a cookie with homemade royal icing, you can start to have so much fun! These are obviously designed to be eaten on a fireworks night, but you can switch the firework theme to anything you fancy – Christmas trees for the festive season, hearts for Valentine's Day or even eggs for Easter. Use the same base cookie recipe and just swap the shapes and colours of the royal icing. Experiment with these and get the family to help you decorate!

MAKES: 10+
PREP: 20 minutes
BAKE: 8–10 minutes
COOL: 30 minutes
DECORATE: 4 hours
LASTS: 3–4+ days,
at room temperature

250g unsalted butter, at room
   temperature
200g caster sugar
1 egg
1 tsp vanilla extract
425g plain flour, plus extra for
   dusting

Icing
2 egg whites
400g icing sugar
½ tsp liquid glucose
½ tsp lemon juice

Decoration
Black, red, yellow, blue food
   colouring, and more colours
   of your choice
Edible glitter (optional)

Preheat the oven to 200°C/180°C fan and line 3–4 baking trays with parchment paper.

In a large bowl, cream together the butter and sugar until light and fluffy. Gradually add the egg and vanilla extract, beating continuously so that the mixture is smooth. Add the flour and beat again until well combined.

Turn the dough out onto a lightly floured work surface and roll out to ½cm thick. Using a 6cm star-shaped cutter, cut out the cookies. Put the cookies onto the lined baking trays spaced a couple of centimetres apart and bake in the oven for 8–10 minutes until they start to turn golden around the edges. Leave to cool on a wire rack.

Icing

Using a clean bowl and whisk (otherwise the egg whites won't stiffen), add the egg whites to the bowl and whisk until stiff peaks form. Gradually add the icing sugar, whisking continuously until well combined. Add the liquid glucose and lemon juice to the mixture and whisk again until the icing is thick and stiff peaks form.

Decoration

Divide the icing into several bowls. (I coloured one-third of the mixture dark blue, left one-third uncoloured and split the rest into small bowls of red, yellow and light blue.)

Outline the cookies with either the black or uncoloured icing and fill with more of the same colour (this is done most easily using a piping bag). Leave the icing to harden and 'set' for 1–2 hours. Once set, use the other colours you created to draw lines, dots, stars or any shapes that look like fireworks. Once more, leave the icing to set. Sprinkle each cookie with a little edible glitter if you fancy.

BIRTHDAY CAKE COOKIES

When you think of a birthday, what springs to mind? I envisage lots of colour, balloons and loads of food. These cookies are meant to represent all of that and I think they work! Two delicious vanilla cookies laced with brightly coloured sprinkles and white chocolate, sandwiched together with a bright buttercream frosting. If you want to make a chocolate cookie dough, you can remove 50g plain flour from the recipe and add 35g cocoa powder instead. Use any colour buttercream you want in the middle – think red or green for Christmas or lilac for Easter... it's up to you!

MAKES: 8
PREP: 20 minutes
CHILL: 30–60 minutes
BAKE: 10–11 minutes
COOL: 30 minutes
FILL: 30 minutes
LASTS: 3–4+ days, at room temperature

115g unsalted butter, at room temperature
100g soft light brown sugar
100g white granulated sugar
1 egg
1 tsp vanilla extract
300g plain flour
½ tsp bicarbonate of soda
½ tsp sea salt
250g white chocolate chips
75g funfetti sprinkles

Filling

75g unsalted butter, at room temperature
150g icing sugar
Pink food colouring

In a large bowl, cream the butter, brown sugar and white sugar together until smooth. Add the egg and vanilla extract and beat again. Add the flour, bicarbonate of soda and sea salt, then beat until a dough is formed. Add the chocolate chips and funfetti sprinkles and mix until well distributed.

Portion the dough out into 16 balls – each should weigh about 60g. Lay the balls out onto a flat tray that fits in the freezer and freeze for at least 30 minutes, or chill in the fridge for an hour or so.

Meanwhile, preheat the oven to 180°C/160°C fan and line three baking trays with parchment paper. Remove the balls from the freezer or fridge and put them onto the lined baking trays. I do roughly six cookies per tray. Bake in the oven for 10–11 minutes. Leave to cool on the trays while you make the filling.

Filling

In a large bowl, beat the butter for a few minutes to loosen it. Add the icing sugar and beat again until smooth. Add a few drops of food colouring (I used pink, but you can use any!) and beat well.

Transfer the pink filling to a piping bag with the piping nozzle of your choice fitted and pipe over eight of the cookies. Sandwich the cookies together with the remaining eight cookies.

HALLOWEEN SANDWICH COOKIES

We all love a nostalgic jam-filled sandwich biscuit, right? So why not make other versions using different shapes like Christmas-themed trees or reindeer? Or maybe baby-shower-themed cookies? I absolutely couldn't resist making some pumpkin- and bat-shaped sandwich cookies for Halloween and these shapes and flavours have got me hooked! A simple, sweet sugar cookie dough, coloured appropriately for orange pumpkins and black bats, sandwiched together with some marmalade makes the perfect treat for serving up at a Halloween party. Using cookie cutters of the same shape, but different sizes makes the sandwiching process so easy.

MAKES: 12–16
PREP: 20 minutes
CHILL: 1+ hours
BAKE: 20 minutes
COOL: 30 minutes
LASTS: 3–4+ days,
at room temperature

250g unsalted butter, at room
   temperature
150g icing sugar
1 tsp vanilla extract
350g plain flour, plus extra
   for dusting
2 egg yolks
1 tsp orange food colouring
1 tsp black food colouring
200g marmalade

In a large bowl, cream together the butter and icing sugar until smooth and combined. Add the vanilla extract, flour and egg yolks and beat again to form a dough.

Divide the dough into two. Colour one batch with the orange food colouring and the other with the black food colouring. Wrap each batch of dough in clingfilm and chill in the fridge for at least 1 hour.

Preheat the oven to 180°C/160°C fan and line four large baking trays with parchment paper. Remove the dough from the fridge and roll out both batches of dough on a lightly floured work surface to roughly ½cm thick. Cut out 6–8 shapes from each batch – I used pumpkin-shaped cutters for the orange dough and bat-shaped cutters for the black dough. Using a smaller cutter of the same shape, cut out another little shape in the middle of each cookie so that the marmalade will be visible once assembled. There should be both orange and black dough left over, so reserve to use later.

Divide the cookies between two of the lined trays and bake in the oven for 10 minutes.

Using the reserved dough, cut out 6–8 more shapes from each batch, without cutting out the middles this time. While the first batch of cookies are cooling on their trays, transfer the second batch to the remaining two lined trays and bake in the oven for 10 minutes. Leave the biscuits to cool on the baking trays.

Take the solid cookies and place a teaspoon of marmalade into the centre, spreading it out over the cookie, but not right to the edge. Sandwich the other cookies with the holes in on top, so they are aligned.

MINI EGG NYC COOKIES

Thick, chunky and sweet New-York-style Mini Egg NYC Cookies stuffed with chocolate chips and chocolate mini eggs... the be-all and end-all of Easter treats! These cookies are without doubt one of the most popular recipes on my blog, and I am not even slightly shocked. Stuff a giant cookie with some of the best Easter chocolates that exist, and you are onto a winner. However, if you wanted to make these at another time of year, such as Christmas, you could use red and green coated chocolates instead. These beauties make a wonderful homemade gift; imagine receiving a few of them in a bag, wrapped with a cute Easter-themed ribbon!

MAKES: 8
PREP: 20 minutes
CHILL: 30–60 minutes
BAKE: 12–14 minutes
COOL: 30+ minutes
LASTS: 3–4+ days, at room temperature

125g unsalted butter, at room temperature
100g soft light brown sugar
75g white granulated sugar
1 egg
1 tsp vanilla extract
300g plain flour
1½ tsp baking powder
½ tsp bicarbonate of soda
½ tsp sea salt
100g milk chocolate chips
250g sugar-coated chocolate mini eggs, chopped (I use Cadbury Mini Eggs)
50g sugar-coated chocolate mini eggs, whole

In a large bowl, cream the butter, brown sugar and white sugar together until smooth. Add the egg and vanilla extract and beat again. Add the flour, baking powder, bicarbonate of soda and sea salt and beat until a dough is formed.

Add the chocolate chips and chopped mini eggs and mix until well distributed.

Portion the dough out into 8 balls (each should weigh about 120g) and lay out onto a flat tray that fits into your freezer. Once rolled into balls, add a few whole mini eggs to each cookie. Put the balls into the freezer for at least 30 minutes, or in the fridge to chill for an hour or so.

Meanwhile, preheat the oven to 200°C/180°C fan and line two baking trays with parchment paper. Remove the balls from the freezer or fridge and transfer them to the lined baking trays (I do four cookies per tray). Bake in the oven for 12–14 minutes. Leave to cool on the trays for at least 30 minutes as they will continue to bake while cooling.

Traybakes

PEANUT BUTTER JELLY BLONDIES

We all know that peanut butter and jam work together exquisitely as a combination and I love the way Americans refer to jam as 'jelly', so I couldn't resist coming up with this recipe. Adding peanut butter, white chocolate chips, raspberries, jam and peanuts to a blondie seemed like an obvious opportunity to create an iconic bake, and so many of you wanted to see this recipe. I think they could be served at a summer party or a birthday as a special dessert, but if we're being honest, these would taste delicious every day of the week.

MAKES: 16
PREP: 20 minutes
BAKE: 25–30 minutes
COOL/SET: 2+ hours
LASTS: 4–5+ days, at room temperature

200g unsalted butter, melted
125g white granulated sugar
125g soft light brown sugar
3 eggs
1 tsp vanilla extract
275g plain flour
1 tbsp cornflour
100g peanuts
100g white chocolate chips
100g fresh raspberries
100g raspberry jam
100g smooth peanut butter

Preheat the oven to 180°C/160°C fan and line a 23cm square tin with parchment paper.

In a large bowl, add the melted butter, white sugar and brown sugar and beat until smooth. Add the eggs and vanilla extract and beat again until smooth. Add the flour and cornflour and beat until thick. Add the peanuts, chocolate chips and raspberries to the mixture and fold through.

Pour the mixture into the tin and spread out evenly. Dollop on the jam and peanut butter using a teaspoon and lightly swirl through the blondie mixture. Bake in the oven for 25–30 minutes, or until there is a slight wobble in the middle. Leave to cool in the tin, then chill in the fridge for at least 2 hours, but preferably overnight. Cut into squares with a sharp knife.

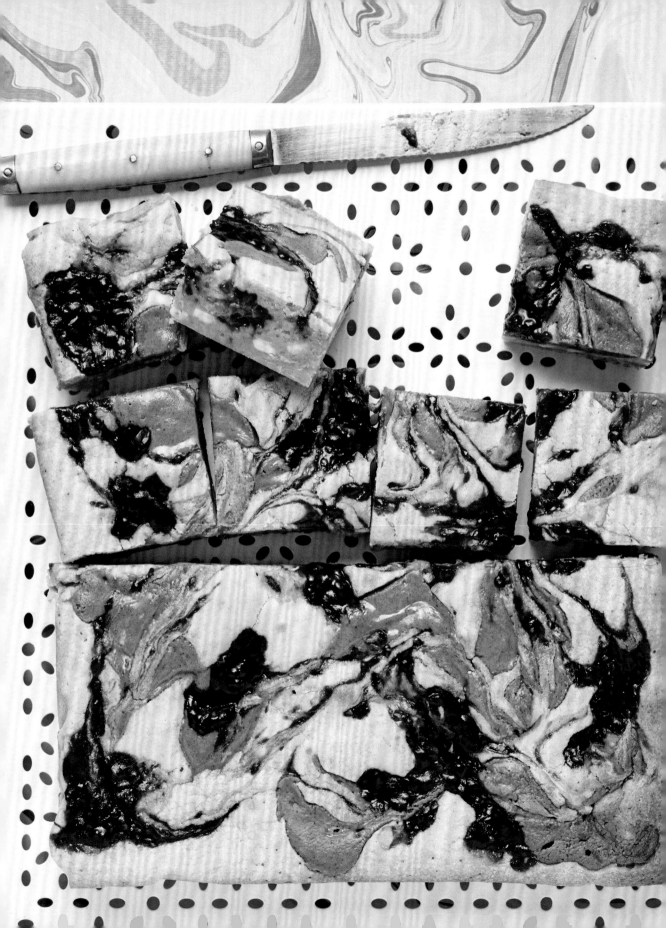

CINNAMON BLONDIES

You may have gathered if you previously made my Peanut Butter Jelly Blondies (page 136) that I am obsessed with all things 'blondie' and these Cinnamon Blondies hit the spot. With my first book and my blog, I was inspired by the ideas that my followers gave me and these have been one of the most highly requested bakes ever, so I had to include them here! An easy blondie batter flavoured with ground cinnamon and stuffed full of white chocolate chips, topped with a cinnamon-flavoured white chocolate drizzle; what could possibly be better? The warmth of the cinnamon makes these ideal for serving at bonfire night or even into the festive period. If you want to try a different spice such as ground ginger, go for it.

MAKES: 16
PREP: 20 minutes
BAKE: 25–30 minutes
COOL: 3+ hours
LASTS: 4–5+ days, at room temperature

200g unsalted butter, melted
250g soft light brown sugar
3 eggs
1 tsp vanilla extract
275g plain flour
3 tsp ground cinnamon
1 tbsp cornflour
300g white chocolate chips
75g white chocolate, melted

Preheat the oven to 180°C/160°C fan and line a 23cm square tin with parchment paper.

In a large bowl, add the melted butter and the sugar and beat until smooth. Add the eggs and vanilla extract and beat again until smooth. Add the flour, 2 teaspoons of cinnamon and the cornflour and beat until thick. Add the chocolate chips and fold through.

Pour the mixture into the tin and spread out evenly. Bake in the oven for 25–30 minutes, or until there is a slight wobble in the middle. Leave to cool in the tin. Chill in the fridge for at least 2 hours, but preferably overnight.

Once the blondies have set, carefully mix the melted white chocolate and remaining 1 teaspoon of cinnamon together. Drizzle over the blondies and return to the fridge to chill and set. Cut into squares with a sharp knife and enjoy!

RICE CRISPY BARS

Rice Crispy Bars are one of those bakes that I think are a necessity for any kid's party – they can be flavoured so easily, you can top them with whatever you want and they are very forgiving, so you can have fun with them! They are sticky, messy and can cause a bit of chaos when making them, but that is part of their charm. Why not make these with your friends or get your kids involved? One tip I can give you is to slightly butter your hands when pressing the mixture into the tin so that it doesn't stick to you. Experiment with different flavours and try topping with a spread of your choice, or even mix 200g of spread into the rice crispy mix itself.

MAKES: 16
PREP: 30 minutes
SET: 2+ hours
LASTS: 4–5+ days,
at room temperature

50g unsalted butter
275g mini marshmallows
  (I use white)
150g rice pops
200g milk chocolate
100g white chocolate

Line a 23cm square tin with parchment paper.

In a large pan, add the butter and mini marshmallows and heat over a low-medium heat, stirring, until smooth and melted. Once melted, remove the pan from the heat and pour the rice pops in, stirring to combine.

Press the mixture into the base of the lined tin (top tip, buttering your hands slightly can prevent any sticking and makes it easy to press down!).

In a small heatproof bowl, break up the milk chocolate into pieces and melt in the microwave in short bursts, stirring well until smooth.

In a separate small heatproof bowl, break up the white chocolate into pieces and melt in the microwave in short bursts, stirring well until smooth.

Pour the melted milk chocolate and white chocolate over the rice pop base and swirl together with a cake skewer, creating a marbled effect. Chill in the fridge for at least 2 hours until set, and then slice into squares with a sharp knife and enjoy!

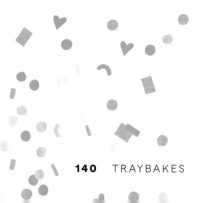

RED VELVET BROWNIES

Red velvet is quite an iconic bake these days, most coffee shops will have a glorious red velvet cake on display and I am not complaining. In my eyes, the perfect red velvet is a balance of chocolate and vanilla, so I decided to experiment with those flavours and my Red Velvet Brownies were born! Brownies lend themselves well to different flavourings, and to up the fun factor I added in a swirl of vanilla cheesecake mix because I just cannot resist cheesecake as you all know! It's so important to use a strong, good-quality red food colouring when you make these (otherwise they will just remain brown) but the finished result is worth it, I promise!

MAKES: 16
PREP: 15 minutes
BAKE: 28–32 minutes
COOL: 1 hour
LASTS: 4–5+ days,
at room temperature

150g unsalted butter, at room
   temperature
350g caster sugar
3 tsp vanilla extract
1 tsp good-quality red food
   colouring (I use Sugarflair)
4 eggs
30g cocoa powder
125g plain flour
1 tsp white wine vinegar
250g full-fat soft cheese
1 egg yolk

Preheat the oven to 180°C/160°C fan and line a 23cm square tin with parchment paper.

In a large bowl, cream the butter and 275g of the sugar together until combined. Add 2 teaspoons of the vanilla extract and the red food colouring and mix well. Add the eggs one at a time, beating after each addition. Add the cocoa powder and flour and beat again. Finally, add the white wine vinegar – mix as little as possible at this point.

In a separate bowl, add the soft cheese, the remaining 75g of sugar and the remaining 1 teaspoon of vanilla extract and beat until smooth. Add the egg yolk and mix again.

Pour 90% of the brownie mixture into the tin – dollop over the cheesecake mixture and then dollop over the remaining brownie mixture. Swirl the mixtures together slightly with a cake skewer and bake in the oven for 28–32 minutes until there is still a slight wobble in the middle of the tin. Leave to cool in the tin for 20–30 minutes and then turn out onto a wire rack to cool fully before cutting into 16 squares with a sharp knife.

MALT CHOCOLATE MILLIONAIRES

Malt chocolate, malt biscuit, caramel... and more. This sumptuous bake is one of my blog favourites and definitely deserves a place in this book. Unlike my Chocolate Orange Millionaire's Shortbread (pages 146–7), this is technically a no-bake version. If you don't fancy using your oven, but still want a delicious treat, you can have this – you just need to make sure those biscuit crumbs are really finely blitzed in the food processor and pressed into the bottom of the tin firmly. The caramel is easy as always, just trust in the process. If you don't want a malt chocolate theme though, just switch to any other biscuit or chocolate of your choice.

MAKES: 16
PREP: 45 minutes
BAKE: 15 minutes
COOL/SET: 3+ hours
LASTS: 4–5+ days, at room temperature

Base

500g malted milk biscuits
200g unsalted butter, melted

Caramel

397g tin condensed milk
200g unsalted butter
3 tbsp caster sugar
4 tbsp golden syrup

Decoration

400g milk chocolate
200g chocolate malt balls
(I use Maltesers), some whole
and some crushed

Base

Line a 23cm square tin with parchment paper.

In a food processor, blitz the biscuits to a fine crumb and add the melted butter – either pulse a few times until the mixture is combined or mix by hand in a bowl.

Tip the biscuit mixture into the tin and press down firmly.

Caramel

In a large pan, add the condensed milk, butter, sugar and golden syrup and melt over a medium heat until the sugar has dissolved, stirring continuously to stop it from catching. Once the sugar has dissolved, increase the heat to high and let the mixture come to boiling point. Boil for 5–7 minutes, stirring continuously. The mixture is ready when it has turned slightly darker golden in colour and has thickened to a soft fudgy texture.

Pour the caramel over the biscuit base and chill in the fridge for 1–2 hours until set.

Decoration

In a small heatproof bowl, break up the milk chocolate into pieces and melt in the microwave in short bursts, or set the bowl over a pan of simmering water (bain-marie) until smooth.

Spread the melted chocolate over the caramel layer and sprinkle over whole and crushed chocolate malt balls. Return to the fridge to chill until set. Cut into squares with a sharp knife and enjoy!

CHOCOLATE ORANGE MILLIONAIRE'S SHORTBREAD

So yeah... a chocolate-orange themed millionaire's shortbread anyone? You will know and love my regular millionaire's shortbread if you have followed me for a while, but this version is on a whole new level. Using orange zest to flavour the shortbread and topping the bake with some orange-flavoured chocolate and a swirl of white chocolate... oh my days! Using orange in the bake is optional, or use an alternative flavouring extract instead. You could base your theme around the caramel layer, using caramel-centred chocolates to decorate. It's up to you, but however you choose to flavour this traybake, its decadence makes it the best Christmas bake ever!

MAKES: 16
PREP: 15 minutes
BAKE: 25–30 minutes
COOL/SET: 3+ hours
DECORATE: 10 minutes
LASTS: 4–5+ days, at room temperature

Base

200g unsalted butter, at room
    temperature
100g caster sugar
275g plain flour
Zest of 2 oranges

Caramel

397g tin condensed milk
200g unsalted butter
3 tbsp caster sugar
4 tbsp golden syrup

Decoration

300g chocolate orange slices
    (I use Terry's), melted
75g white chocolate, melted
16 chocolate orange slices,
    to decorate

Base

Preheat the oven to 180°C/160°C fan and line a 23cm square tin with parchment paper.

In a large bowl, cream the butter and sugar together until smooth. Add the flour and orange zest and beat again until a dough is formed. Firmly press the dough into the bottom of the tin and bake in the oven for 25–30 minutes until pale golden on top. Remove from the oven and leave to cool.

Caramel

In a large pan, add the condensed milk, butter, sugar and golden syrup and melt over a medium heat until the sugar has dissolved, stirring frequently to stop the mixture from catching. Once the sugar has fully dissolved, increase the heat to high and let the mixture come to boiling point. Boil for 5–7 minutes, stirring continuously. The mixture is ready when it has turned a slightly darker golden colour and has thickened to a soft fudgy texture.

Pour the caramel over the shortbread base and chill in the fridge for 1 hour until set.

Decoration

In a small heatproof bowl, melt the chocolate orange slices in short bursts in the microwave. Pour the melted chocolate orange slices over the chilled caramel. Drizzle the melted white chocolate over the chocolate orange layer to form a pretty pattern or simply drizzle over.

Place the 16 chocolate orange slices equally spaced on top of the swirled layer. Return to the fridge for another 1–2 hours to chill, until the chocolate has set. Chop the shortbread into 16 slices with a sharp knife, using the chocolate orange slices as a guide and enjoy.

VALENTINE'S COOKIE BARS

There is something about eating a cookie bar that is so much more fun than eating a regular-shaped cookie and this recipe creates the cutest bars. I adore a flavour theme when it comes to my cookie bars, but when you can theme them colour-wise as I have done here, they look even more amazing. I enjoy giving homemade gifts at any time of year, but around Valentine's Day it just seems so appropriate to bake something with love for your other half, or for friends if you like to celebrate with your pals. As always, it would be easy to match the theme colours to any other celebration – Christmas, Easter or even a birthday.

MAKES: 16
PREP: 15 minutes
BAKE: 20–22 minutes
COOL: 30 minutes
LASTS: 4–5+ days,
at room temperature

275g plain flour
1 tsp bicarbonate of soda
½ tsp sea salt
1 tbsp cornflour
115g unsalted butter
100g white granulated sugar
100g soft light brown sugar
1 egg
1 tsp vanilla extract
250g milk chocolate chunks
250g red/white/pink chocolates

Preheat the oven to 190°C/170°C fan and line a 23cm square tin with parchment paper.

In a large bowl, whisk together the flour, bicarbonate of soda, sea salt and cornflour. Leave to one side.

In a small bowl, melt the butter in the microwave in short bursts. Add the melted butter, white sugar and brown sugar to a large bowl and whisk together for 2 minutes until the sugars start to dissolve and the mixture becomes smooth. Add the egg and the vanilla extract and briefly whisk again until combined.

Add the reserved dry ingredients to the wet mixture and beat until a thick cookie dough is formed. Add the chocolate chunks and the coloured chocolates and mix well to distribute evenly through the dough. Press the cookie dough into the bottom of the tin and bake in the oven for 20–22 minutes until golden in colour.

Leave the mixture to cool in the tin for 10 minutes and then turn out onto a wire rack and cool fully. Cut into 16 squares with a sharp knife and enjoy!

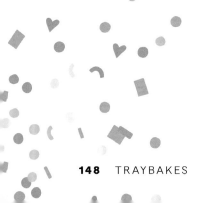

EASTER FLAPJACKS

Butter, sugar, golden syrup and oats create one of the most classic and easiest bakes in the world, the beloved flapjack. Messing with the tradition of this bake is pure fun – add a load of Easter chocolates and even more chocolate chips for the wow factor! Kids will love these – you can use their favourite chocolates or you can also leave the chocolate out for a great basic flapjack. These are undeniably one of those crowd-pleaser traybakes and will disappear within seconds as they are such a nostalgic and familiar treat.

MAKES: 16
PREP: 15 minutes
BAKE: 20–25 minutes
COOL/SET: 2 hours
LASTS: 4–5+ days,
at room temperature

200g unsalted butter
200g soft light brown sugar
200g golden syrup
400g rolled oats
100g milk chocolate chips
200g Easter chocolates

Topping
100g milk chocolate, melted
100g Easter chocolates, chopped

Preheat the oven to 180°C/160°C fan and line a 23cm square tin with parchment paper.

In a medium pan, add the butter, sugar and golden syrup and melt over a low heat until smooth. Leave to cool for about 5 minutes.

In a large bowl, add the rolled oats, chocolate chips and Easter chocolates and mix well. Pour the butter mixture over and stir to combine. Firmly press the mixture into the base of the tin and bake in the oven for 20–25 minutes until it starts to brown around the edges and firm up. Leave to cool fully in the tin.

Topping
Carefully drizzle the melted milk chocolate over the flapjacks while they are in the tin. Scatter over the Easter chocolates, then chill the flapjacks in the fridge. Cut into squares with a sharp knife and enjoy.

COSY HOT CHOCOLATE BROWNIES

If you know me or have followed my Jane's Patisserie journey for long enough, you will know how hot chocolate obsessed I am! This is a year-round obsession for me, but I am 100% more in the mood once the weather has started turning autumnal and adding that comforting flavour to a brownie is even better. Imagine a classic chocolate brownie base, but with the addition of a good-quality (made from milk) hot chocolate powder, chocolate chips and marshmallow fluff... oh my. I take these brownies even further with a chocolate ganache topping, a sprinkling of marshmallows and chocolate flake pieces and a final dusting of hot chocolate powder, because why not? Autumn, winter, whenever... these will keep you cosy all year round, so give them a go!

MAKES: 16
PREP: 30 minutes
BAKE: 25–30 minutes
COOL/SET: 2½ hours
LASTS: 4–5+ days, at room temperature

200g unsalted butter

200g dark chocolate

4 eggs

275g caster sugar

75g plain flour

75g good-quality hot chocolate powder

150g milk chocolate chips

200g marshmallow fluff

Ganache

75g dark chocolate

75g milk chocolate

150ml double cream

Preheat the oven to 180°C/160°C fan and line a 23cm square tin with parchment paper.

In a large heatproof bowl, add the butter and dark chocolate and melt in the microwave in short bursts or heat over a pan of simmering water until melted. Leave to cool for 5 minutes.

In a separate large bowl, whisk together the eggs and sugar for a few minutes until the colour has turned pale and the whisk leaves a trail of mixture when lifted out. Once whisked, pour the cooled chocolate mixture over the eggs and fold together carefully. It might take some time, but be patient – you do not want to knock out the air you previously incorporated.

Once fully combined, sift the flour and hot chocolate powder into the chocolate mixture and gently fold together once more. Fold through the chocolate chips and pour the mixture into the lined tin. Dollop in the marshmallow fluff and swirl through ever so slightly.

Bake in the oven for 25–30 minutes. Leave to cool fully in the tin. Then, chill in the fridge for at least 2 hours.

Ganache

Once the brownies have chilled and set, make the ganache. Add the dark chocolate, milk chocolate and double cream to a small heatproof jug and melt in the microwave in short bursts, stirring until smooth. Spread the ganache over the brownies.

Decoration

50g mini marshmallows

50g marshmallows

100g chocolate flake, chopped

Hot chocolate powder, for dusting

Decoration

Scatter the mini marshmallows and regular marshmallows over the ganache, along with the chopped chocolate flake pieces. Sprinkle over a dusting of hot chocolate powder.

Chill in the fridge for at least 30 minutes. Cut into squares with a sharp knife and enjoy.

MINCE PIE BROWNIES

Mince pies are one of the most iconic British bakes, but to break from tradition slightly, I thought I would have fun by merging them with another iconic bake – the brownie. Introducing the pastry-bottomed, mince pie-stuffed brownie! You can cheat and use shop-bought pastry if you wish, but making it yourself is surprisingly easy, give it a go. If you want to make your own mincemeat, you can find a great recipe on my blog. These hybrid goodies are a magical match made in heaven and perfect for the festive season.

MAKES: 16
PREP: 1 hour
BAKE: 1 hour
COOL: 4 hours
LASTS: 4–5+ days, at room temperature

Base

265g plain flour, plus extra for dusting
2 tbsp icing sugar
150g chilled unsalted butter, cubed, plus extra for greasing
2 egg yolks
2 tbsp cold water

Brownies

200g dark chocolate
200g unsalted butter
4 eggs
275g soft light brown sugar
100g plain flour
50g cocoa powder
600g mincemeat

Base

Grease and flour the inside of a 23cm square tin.

In a large bowl, sift the flour and icing sugar. Add the butter, egg yolks and cold water and rub the mixture together with your fingertips until it resembles breadcrumbs. Bring it all together with your hands and knead until a smooth pastry is formed.

Turn out the pastry onto a lightly floured surface and roll out into a large square shape until 3–4mm thick. Press the pastry into the bottom and sides of the tin and trim and neaten the edges if necessary. Chill in the fridge for 30 minutes.

Meanwhile, preheat the oven to 200°C/180°C fan.

Cover the pastry with parchment paper and fill with baking beans or rice and bake the pastry 'blind' for 20 minutes. Remove the parchment paper and the beans and bake for an extra 10 minutes or until the pastry is cooked through and turning golden in colour. Leave to cool in the tin.

Brownies

Reduce the oven temperature to 180°C/160°C fan.

In a small heatproof bowl, break up the chocolate into pieces, add the butter and melt in short bursts in the microwave, or over a pan of simmering water (bain-marie). Leave to cool for 5 minutes.

In a large bowl, whisk together the eggs and sugar for a few minutes until the colour has turned pale and the whisk leaves trails of mixture when lifted out. Pour the cooled chocolate mixture over the egg mixture and fold together carefully. It might take some time, but be patient – you do not want to knock out the air you previously incorporated. Once fully combined, sift the flour and cocoa powder into the brownie mixture and gently fold together once more.

Spread the mincemeat over the bottom of the pastry case and then pour over the brownie mixture. Bake in the oven for 25–30 minutes. Leave to cool in the tin. Chill in the fridge for at least 2 hours until set. Cut into squares with a sharp knife.

Desserts

IRISH CREAM TART

This dessert is one of the most luxurious no-bake treats you can make. I used digestive biscuits for the base with the addition of cocoa powder to make it extra chocolatey. Alternatively, you could use a chocolate digestive biscuit instead, but you would only need to use 100g of the butter. For the filling, the mix of milk chocolate and dark chocolate gives the ideal balance, especially when paired with the Irish cream liqueur. I serve this every Christmas season as it always goes down well, but you know it would suit a New Year's Eve or a dinner party!

SERVES: 12
PREP: 30 minutes
CHILL: 3 hours
LASTS: 3+ days,
in the fridge

Base

300g digestive biscuits
35g cocoa powder
150g unsalted butter, melted

Filling

175g dark chocolate
175g milk chocolate
50g unsalted butter
300ml double cream
150ml Irish cream liqueur
  (I use Baileys Original)

Topping

125ml double cream
25ml Irish cream liqueur
2 tbsp icing sugar
Grated milk chocolate

Base

In a food processor, blitz the biscuits and cocoa powder to a fine crumb, add the melted butter and pulse a few times until well combined. Transfer to a 23cm loose-bottomed tart tin and press firmly into the base and sides.

Filling

In a large bowl, add the dark chocolate, milk chocolate and butter. In a small pan, add the double cream and Irish cream liqueur and heat until just before boiling point. Pour over the chocolate and butter and whisk together until smooth.

Pour the filling into the biscuit crust and chill in the fridge for around 3 hours until set.

Topping

Carefully remove the biscuit crust from the tin and transfer to a serving plate.

In a large bowl, whip the double cream, Irish cream liqueur and icing sugar together to form soft peaks. Transfer to a piping bag with a piping nozzle fitted and pipe swirls over the tart. Grate some chocolate over the dessert before serving.

BLACK FOREST PAVLOVA

If you know me, you will know that meringues are on my list of top desserts. Although surprisingly easy to make, meringues always look like showstoppers and when you add one of the most retro flavour combinations ever to the mix, you get this fabulous creation... YUM! This dessert is slightly life changing and it is IDEAL for Christmas festivities and would look fabulous at the centre of any dinner party table. Lighter than a traditional Black Forest gateau because of the meringue base, it's the perfect dessert after a heavy meal when you're craving something sweet, but don't think you have enough room left.

SERVES: 12
PREP: 30 minutes
BAKE: 1 hour
COOL: 3 hours
DECORATE: 30 minutes
LASTS: 1–2+ days,
in the fridge

6 egg whites
275g caster sugar
45g cocoa powder
½ tsp vanilla extract
1 tsp white wine vinegar

Decoration

450ml double cream
2 tbsp icing sugar
250g cherry pie filling
250g cherries soaked in kirsch
Fresh cherries
Chocolate shavings

Preheat the oven to 150°C/130°C fan. Line a large square baking tray with baking parchment.

Using a clean bowl and whisk (otherwise the egg whites won't stiffen), add the egg whites to the bowl and whisk until stiff peaks form. Start adding 1 teaspoon of sugar at a time, while continuously whisking, until all of the sugar has been incorporated and the mixture is glossy.

Sieve in the cocoa powder and add the vanilla extract and white wine vinegar to the egg white mixture. Fold in with a large spatula as carefully as you can until smooth and combined.

Using a small dab of meringue mixture in each corner, stick the parchment paper to the baking tray. Spoon the meringue onto the tray, creating a large circular shape (the meringue will spread slightly when baking so don't go right to the edge of the baking tray!). Bake in the oven for 1 hour – turn the oven off and leave to cool completely, without opening the door, for about 3 hours.

Decoration

In a large bowl, whip the double cream with the icing sugar.

In a separate bowl, mix together the cherry pie filling and the cherries soaked in kirsch. Alternatively, use cherry jam if you don't want alcohol, fresh cherries, or anything similar.

Dollop the whipped cream onto the meringue and then add the cherry mixture on top. Add some fresh cherries for decoration and sprinkle over some chocolate shavings.

RASPBERRY PROSECCO TRIFLE

An exquisitely boozy raspberry and prosecco trifle ideal for New Year's Eve celebrations or any time you need a little lift – what could be better? Prosecco, sponge fingers, raspberries, vanilla custard and more. I feel like since starting my blog, I am always expected to bring cake to a party, and I can understand why! However, sometimes when you want a little more time to get ready for the party itself, making something like this ahead of time that requires so little effort is a cinch. Literally, whacking it all together in a large trifle bowl with a drizzle and a sip (cook's perks!) of prosecco here and there couldn't be easier. Of course, if you want to make a non-alcoholic raspberry trifle, you can leave out the prosecco, or swap it for lemon juice to contrast nicely with the fresh raspberries.

SERVES: 15
PREP: 1 hour +
overnight
SET: 3+ hours
LASTS: 2–3 days,
in the fridge

350g fresh raspberries
600ml prosecco
600ml double cream
75g icing sugar
200g sponge fingers
300g raspberry jam
500ml vanilla custard

Topping
Fresh raspberries
Freeze-dried raspberries
Sprinkles

Soak the raspberries in 250ml of the prosecco, cover with clingfilm and chill overnight in the fridge.

Carefully boil 250ml of the remaining prosecco in a pan (or use the prosecco that has been drained from the raspberries instead, like I do) until it reduces to about 50ml. Leave to cool.

In a large bowl, whip the double cream with the icing sugar until soft peaks form. Add the prosecco syrup, and mix to combine. Chill in the fridge.

At the bottom of a large trifle bowl, add one-third of the sponge fingers and drizzle over some of the remaining 100ml of prosecco. Spread some jam over the top and then add some of the reserved prosecco-soaked raspberries. Pour over one-third of the custard and then dollop on one-third of the whipped prosecco cream.

Repeat the layers again – sponge with drizzle, jam, raspberries, custard and then the cream. If you are doing three layers like me, repeat again!

Topping
Decorate with some fresh raspberries, some freeze-dried raspberries and some sprinkles.

Leave to chill in the fridge for a few hours before serving.

CHOCOLATE FONDANTS

We have all eaten a chocolate fondant, with its rich molten middle oozing out, right? The perception is that this is a really-hard-to-make-perfectly pudding, but don't be scared off, my recipe is easy. This is the perfect dessert for Valentine's Day, or any other time you want to make something gooey and chocolatey for loved ones. Double or triple the quantities in the recipe to serve more people at a dinner party and impress your friends. The key to fondant success is to make sure your oven is at the correct temperature (an oven thermometer is your best friend in the baking world) and to hold your nerve when it comes to timing. Serve with a dollop of ice cream or even some chilled double cream... luxurious heaven!

SERVES: 2
PREP: 30 minutes
CHILL: 15 minutes
BAKE: 11–13 minutes
LASTS: 1 day (but best served fresh)

15g unsalted butter, melted, for brushing

15g cocoa powder, for dusting

50g dark chocolate

50g unsalted butter

50g soft light brown sugar

1 medium egg

1 medium egg yolk

50g plain flour

Using a pastry brush, brush melted butter all over the inside of two 8cm pudding moulds. Dust the insides with cocoa powder, shaking about to make sure the cocoa powder covers all the melted butter.

In a small heatproof bowl, break the dark chocolate into pieces and add the butter. Melt in the microwave in short bursts or set the bowl over a pan of simmering water (bain-marie). Leave to cool completely.

In a separate small bowl, add the sugar, egg and egg yolk and whisk until thick and pale and the whisk leaves a trail when you lift it out of the mixture. Add the flour and mix in. Then, add the cooled chocolate mixture and mix until fully combined. The mixture should be quite runny.

Divide the mixture equally between the two moulds and chill in the fridge for 15 minutes.

Meanwhile, preheat the oven to 200°C/180°C fan. Bake the fondants in the oven for 11–13 minutes until the mixture starts to slightly come away from the edge of the moulds and the tops are firm. Leave the fondants to sit for a couple of minutes in the moulds before turning out onto serving plates.

CHAMPAGNE RASPBERRY POSSETS

One of the most popular bakes from my first book was my lemon posset tart – it's so easy to make, has a beautifully sharp yet sweet flavour and a heavenly creamy texture. For this version, I thought I would take it up a notch and create these individual celebratory desserts to enjoy in the summertime or at a birthday party. With a homemade raspberry champagne sauce, fresh raspberries and cream, these luxurious possets deserve to be savoured. You can of course swap the berries for strawberries or use prosecco instead of champagne.

SERVES: 4
PREP: 1 hour
SET: 4–5 hours
LASTS: 1–2+ days, in the fridge

275g fresh raspberries
65ml champagne
225ml double cream
75g caster sugar

Decoration

Leftover raspberry champagne sauce
50g fresh raspberries

In a small pan, add 175g raspberries and the champagne and heat over a medium heat until the raspberries start to break down. Add the mixture to a blender and blend until smooth. Sieve the mixture to remove the seeds of the raspberries and leave to cool fully.

In a medium pan, add the double cream and sugar. Heat over a low heat, slowly letting the sugar dissolve into the cream. Once the sugar is fully dissolved, increase the heat to medium and stir continuously. When the mixture reaches boiling point, allow it to boil gently for 1–1½ minutes.

Remove the pan from the heat and whisk in most of the reserved raspberry champagne sauce, leaving some in the pan for drizzling later.

Divide the remaining 100g raspberries between four ramekins, and then pour the cream mixture on top of each. Chill in the fridge for 4–5 hours until set.

Decoration

Drizzle the remaining raspberry champagne sauce over the four possets and add a few raspberries to each before serving.

SPECULOOS LAVA CAKES

Just like a chocolate fondant, these are the epitome of gorgeous – individual chocolate cakes, with a molten speculoos centre. Lava cakes are impressive to cut into, a joy to eat and so easy to adjust the recipe to however you like. Speculoos spread (I use Biscoff) is my spread of choice, but you could use chocolate hazelnut spread (I use Nutella), white chocolate spread... you get the idea. It's important to use dark chocolate in the batter of these lava cakes to contrast with the sweetness of the spread in the middle and to create the best balance of flavours.

SERVES: 2
PREP: 1½ hours
BAKE: 15–17 minutes
COOL: 10 minutes
LASTS: 1 day (but best served fresh)

100g speculoos spread (I use Biscoff), plus extra to serve

15g unsalted butter, melted, for brushing

75g dark chocolate

100g unsalted butter

1 egg

2 egg yolks

75g caster sugar

50g plain flour

Freeze the speculoos spread in two dollops on a tray that fits in your freezer, for at least 1 hour.

Using a pastry brush, brush melted butter all over the insides of two 8cm pudding moulds. Dust the insides with cocoa powder, shaking about to make sure the cocoa powder covers all of the melted butter.

Preheat the oven to 210°C/190°C fan.

Break the dark chocolate into pieces and put in a small heatproof bowl with the butter. Heat in the microwave in short bursts or set the bowl over a pan of simmering water (bain-marie) until melted. Leave to cool for 5 minutes.

In a separate bowl, pour in the chocolate mixture and add the egg and egg yolks. Mix until combined. Add the sugar and flour and mix again until well combined.

Divide the mixture equally between the two pudding moulds. Press the frozen dollops of speculoos spread into each mould and bake in the oven for 15–17 minutes until the top of the cakes are firm.

Remove from the oven and let them cool in the moulds for 10 minutes, then turn out onto serving plates. Serve with ice cream and drizzle over some extra speculoos spread.

SALTED CARAMEL CHOC POTS

Smooth salted caramel is probably what most people think of when it comes to an indulgent flavour, and I am one of its biggest fans. Salted caramel anything works for me! Making your own salted caramel sauce takes this recipe to another level and topped with a silky homemade chocolate ganache, you taste heaven in every bite. These pots are rich, but perfectly formed and I prepare them ahead of time to chill in the fridge when my friends are coming over for girls' night or serve them at the end of a dinner party.

SERVES: 8
PREP: 30 minutes
SET: 2–3 hours
LASTS: 2–3+ days, in the fridge

Sauce

150g white granulated sugar

250g white granulated sugar
75ml water
60g unsalted butter
200ml double cream
1 tsp vanilla extract
½ tsp sea salt

Chocolate Pots

150g milk chocolate
150g dark chocolate
200ml double cream
100ml full-fat milk
75g shortbread biscuit crumbs

Sauce

In a large heavy-based pan, add the sugar and water. Heat over a low-medium heat, stirring continuously until the sugar has fully dissolved. Once the mixture starts to bubble slightly, increase the heat to high and STOP STIRRING. Leave the mixture alone, and do not touch it. Wait for the mixture to boil away to an amber colour. This can sometimes take 5–10 minutes, depending on the pan and hob used.

Remove the amber-coloured mixture from the heat and add the butter. The mixture will bubble up quite a bit, but keep whisking it together until combined. Add the double cream, and whisk. Add the vanilla extract and sea salt and whisk until fully combined. Pour into a bowl and leave to cool fully.

Chocolate Pots

In a pan, break up the milk and dark chocolate into pieces and add the double cream and milk. Heat over a low heat, stirring continuously, until the mixture has melted.

Divide the salted caramel sauce equally between eight glasses, then pour the chocolate mixture over the caramel. Chill the pots in the fridge for 2–3 hours. Sprinkle over the shortbread biscuit crumbs and serve.

COOKIES 'N' CREAM ICE CREAM

No-churn ice cream is one of the easiest things you can whip up, especially when you are desperately in the mood for something cold in the summer months... and this dream of a recipe has only three ingredients! All the ingredients are easy to get hold of at any supermarket, or even at your local corner shop. The wonderful thing is that you can use whatever other biscuits you like or that are available to you – custard creams, bourbons or maybe even speculoos biscuits (I use Biscoff) would all work wonderfully. You can even try swapping the biscuits for your favourite chocolate spread.

SERVES: 12
PREP: 15 minutes
FREEZE: 4 hours
LASTS: 3+ months,
in the freezer

600ml double cream

397g tin condensed milk

150g cookies and cream biscuits, crushed to a fine crumb (I use Oreos)

150g cookies and cream biscuits, chopped/quartered

In a large bowl, add the double cream and condensed milk. Whisk until smooth and even. Continue to whisk until the mixture starts to thicken – it doesn't need to be extremely thick, it just needs to be smooth and starting to thicken.

Add the finely crushed biscuits to the cream mixture (I crush them in my food processor, or you can use a bowl with a rolling pin, or a sandwich bag or similar!).

Add one-third of the mixture to a container – I use a 900g loaf tin – and swirl through one-third of the chopped/quartered biscuits. Repeat twice more so that all the biscuits are used up. Put the tin in the freezer until frozen and firm.

EASTER CHOCOLATE MOUSSE

I always think that chocolate mousse is underrated in the dessert world and that it deserves more love. When I was younger, chocolate mousse was one of my favourite things to eat as a snack or a dessert, so a homemade version topped with Easter chocolates is irresistible to me. I used milk chocolate as I wanted something a little lighter, but you can switch it to 150g dark chocolate if you prefer a richer, more sophisticated taste. This recipe works all year round, but top with whatever you prefer to reflect the season or celebration. Truffle chocolates for a birthday, sprinkles for a children's party or fruit for a summer event.

SERVES: 6–8
PREP: 30 minutes
CHILL: 2–3 hours
DECORATE: 10 minutes
LASTS: 1–2+ days,
in the fridge

175g milk chocolate
60ml double cream
5 egg whites
50g caster sugar
25g cocoa powder
100g Easter chocolates, chopped

Decoration

150ml double cream
2 tbsp icing sugar
100g Easter chocolates, some
 chopped, some whole
Milk chocolate shavings

In a medium heatproof bowl, melt the milk chocolate until smooth in the microwave in short bursts or set the bowl over a pan of simmering water (bain-marie). Leave to cool for a few minutes, then add the double cream and beat until thick.

Using a clean bowl and whisk (otherwise the egg whites won't stiffen), add the egg whites to the bowl and whisk until stiff peaks form. Add the sugar 1 teaspoon at a time, while continuously whisking, until all the sugar has been incorporated and the mixture is glossy.

Add 1 heaped tablespoon of the egg white mixture to the chocolate mixture and beat like crazy until combined. Carefully add the rest of the egg white mixture and the cocoa powder to the chocolate mixture and fold together until fully combined. Finally, fold through the chopped Easter chocolates.

Divide the mixture equally between 6–8 glasses and smooth over. Chill in the fridge for 2–3 hours to set.

Decoration

In a medium bowl, whisk the double cream and icing sugar together until smooth. Transfer to a piping bag with a piping nozzle of your choice fitted, pipe the cream onto the chocolate mousses and scatter over the Easter chocolates and some chocolate shavings.

MINCE PIE ICE CREAM

My easy festive Mince Pie Ice Cream recipe is perfect at Christmas time, or for when you want a little taste of Christmas at any other time of year. This recipe starts in a similar way to most of my other no-churn ice cream recipes, with double cream and condensed milk, but it's the addition of chopped mince pies, mincemeat, and a little mixed spice that makes this a truly special companion to any festive pudding or a luxurious dessert in its own right. Why not level up the recipe and bake my Gingerbread Mince Pies (page 202) to stir in? Or try swapping the mixed spice for a little ground ginger or finely chopped stem ginger.

SERVES: 14
PREP: 10 minutes
FREEZE: 4 hours
LASTS: 3+ months, in the freezer

600ml double cream
397g tin condensed milk
1 tsp vanilla extract
½ tsp mixed spice
6 mince pies, chopped (try my Gingerbread Mince Pies, page 202)
200g mincemeat

In a large bowl, add the double cream, condensed milk, vanilla extract and mixed spice. Whisk until smooth and even. Continue to whisk until the mixture starts to thicken – it doesn't need to be extremely thick, it just needs to be smooth and starting to thicken. Alternatively, you can whip the cream in a separate bowl to form soft peaks and then fold the ingredients together.

Add one-third of the mixture to a container – I use a 900g loaf tin – and swirl through two of the chopped mince pies and one-third of the mincemeat. Repeat twice more so that all of the ingredients are used up. Put the tin in the freezer until frozen and firm and enjoy.

CHEAT'S CHRISTMAS PUDDING

Christmas pudding is one of those iconic dishes that, if I'm being honest, is not my favourite thing to make. It's having to remember when to start it, remembering when to feed it, and all sorts... but this pudding recipe? Oh, it's just SO easy and quick to do in comparison! There is no Stir-up Sunday needed – whack all the ingredients together in a bowl, beat until everything is distributed evenly and pour into your prepared pudding basin. Yes, you do need to make sure the basin will fit in the pan you are using to simmer it in (a mistake I made at first), but that's all you need to remember. Serve with a dollop of cream, set alight with a little brandy or even enjoy alongside a chunk of cheese.

SERVES: 12
PREP: 30 minutes
COOK: 2½ hours
LASTS: 2–3+ days, at room temperature

150g raisins

150g sultanas

50g mixed peel

150g self-raising flour

125g chilled unsalted butter, grated

100g fresh breadcrumbs

215g soft light brown sugar

150g mixed nuts

1 tsp ground cinnamon

1 tsp mixed spice

1 tsp ground ginger

250ml full-fat milk

1 egg

In a large bowl, mix the raisins, sultanas, mixed peel, flour, butter, breadcrumbs, sugar, mixed nuts, cinnamon, mixed spice and ginger. Add the milk and egg and beat until well combined.

Grease and line a 1.5L pudding basin with parchment paper and pour in the mixture. Cover the basin with a double layer of buttered foil, making a pleat in the middle so the pudding has room to grow. Secure the foil to the basin with string, and then place into a large pan that will fit the bowl. Pour some boiling water into the pan so that it comes a few centimetres up the sides of the basin, put the pan lid on and let it simmer for 2½ hours, checking the water level every 20–30 minutes. When the water gets lower, top it up slightly so there is always water in the pan.

Carefully remove the steamed pudding from the pan with oven gloves and pour away the hot water. Remove the string and foil and turn the pudding out onto a serving plate. Enjoy!

Sweets *and* Treats

WATERMELON SLUSHIES

When it's peak summer and it's BBQ season, all I ever want is an ice-cold, refreshing drink and this is the recipe I dream of. Three simple ingredients combine to create something thirst- quenching and more than the sum of its parts. I used both frozen and fresh fruit chunks for the right consistency. Prepare and freeze watermelon chunks ahead of time and store in your freezer for when you need them. I added lemon juice to the fresh raspberries to balance the sweetness and bring a little more flavour. Feel free to switch the watermelon for other types of melon to change it up, or substitute the fresh raspberries with other fresh or frozen berries – this is such a versatile recipe, so have fun with it!

SERVES: 3
PREP: 5 minutes
LASTS: Best served fresh

Make sure the chunks of watermelon are fully frozen. In a blender, add the frozen watermelon chunks, the raspberries and lemon juice. Blitz until smooth, pour into glasses and enjoy!

1 small watermelon, in frozen
  chunks
250g fresh raspberries
50ml lemon juice

CHEESECAKE STUFFED STRAWBERRIES

To my mind, there couldn't be a better combination than sweet cheesecake and fragrant strawberries. If you don't have time to make a cheesecake, why not cheat with these quick mouthful-sized bites for an instant hit. Core out a strawberry slightly, stuff it with a whipped cheesecake mixture and sprinkle over some biscuit crumbs for crunch – the best part of a cheesecake if you ask me. I used a vanilla cheesecake filling, but you could try a chocolate one by substituting 25g cocoa powder in place of 25g of the icing sugar. Or dip the strawberries in a little melted chocolate and let it set. An ideal dessert to celebrate Valentine's Day, but I'd devour these at any opportunity!

MAKES: 15
PREP: 1 hour
SET: 1+ hours
LASTS: 1–2+ days, in the fridge

500g strawberries
250g full-fat soft cheese
125g icing sugar
1 tsp vanilla extract
30g biscuit crumbs

Wash and dry the strawberries and cut the tops off carefully. Core out a small amount of each strawberry from the top with a sharp knife.

In a small bowl, mix the soft cheese, icing sugar and vanilla extract until well combined. Transfer the mixture to a piping bag with a piping nozzle fitted and pipe into the cored-out strawberries.

Sprinkle the tops of each strawberry with biscuit crumbs. Chill in the fridge for at least 1 hour to set and enjoy.

SPRINKLE CAKE POPS

Cake pops have become more and more popular over the years because they are fun to make and look cute. You can use any leftover cake you may have, or even a shop-bought cake if that is easier. I love the idea of these as they work for any type of celebration, especially kids' birthdays as the individual portions are neat to eat and can be themed appropriately. I used a leftover vanilla cake and some leftover buttercream – the ratios are the only important part to stick to, otherwise go wild with the flavours. I dipped the cake pops in melted white chocolate and coated them with colourful sprinkles, but you could use milk or dark chocolate to coat them and crushed nuts would make a tasty coating.

MAKES: 30
PREP: 1 hour
SET: 2 hours
LASTS: 1+ weeks,
in the fridge

Roughly 1 x 22cm cake (weighing
about 650g)
Roughly 250g buttercream
400g white chocolate (or candy
melts in a colour of your choice)
50g sprinkles

Line a baking tray with parchment paper.

In a large bowl, break the cake up into crumbs. Add the buttercream and stir together. Using your hands, roll truffle-sized balls of the mixture and place onto the lined baking tray.

Push a lolly/cake pop stick into each ball and put in the freezer for at least 30 minutes or chill in the fridge for 1 hour.

In a small heatproof bowl, break up the white chocolate into pieces and melt in the microwave in short bursts or over a pan of simmering water (bain-marie) until smooth.

In a small bowl, add the sprinkles. Dip each cake pop into the melted chocolate mixture, letting any excess chocolate drip off. Dip into the sprinkles to coat, then stand upright in a mug to set at room temperature or chill in the fridge for 30 minutes until the chocolate has hardened.

HOMEMADE FILLED CREME EGGS

When I think of Easter, I imagine all the recipes I can make and Easter chocolate is one of my favourite things in the world to bake with. I am always bulk buying Easter-themed chocolate as soon as I can find it in the shops, but this made me wonder, why don't I try making my own? Then I can eat filled chocolate eggs all year-round when they aren't in the shops! Each homemade filled egg is about 2.5cm in length, so they are quite small, but perfectly bite-sized. If you have a larger mould than me, just multiply the quantity of the ingredients to fit as chocolate moulds can vary.

MAKES: 15
PREP: 2 hours
COOK: 20 minutes
SET: 3 hours
LASTS: 7+ days, in the fridge

100–150g milk chocolate

55g golden syrup

25g unsalted butter, at room temperature

1 tsp vanilla extract

125g icing sugar

½ tsp yellow food colouring

Get some egg moulds ready – I used two trays of 15 so I had 30 egg halves. Each egg measured about 2.5cm tall in the mould.

In a small heatproof bowl or jug, break the milk chocolate into pieces and melt in the microwave in short bursts or over a pan of simmering water (bain-marie) until smooth.

Carefully pour a small amount of the melted chocolate into the moulds, swirling to coat the insides. Try not to overfill so there is room for the filling. Chill the eggs in the fridge for about 30 minutes to set the first chocolate layer.

Repeat with more of the melted chocolate to create a second chocolate coating and to strengthen the shells. Return to the fridge to chill until firm. Reserve any melted chocolate for later.

In a large bowl, beat the golden syrup, butter and vanilla extract until combined. Add the icing sugar and beat until smooth. Remove one-quarter of the filling and colour with yellow food colouring.

Transfer the white filling to a piping bag with a piping nozzle fitted and fill each chocolate egg two-thirds full.

Transfer the reserved yellow filling to another piping bag and pipe a small amount of the yellow mixture into the middle of the white mixture in each egg half to form a 'yolk'.

see next page

Put the moulds in the freezer for about 2 hours until the filling is frozen. Carefully remove the egg halves from the moulds.

Using any leftover melted milk chocolate (that you may have to re-melt), sandwich two halves together to make a whole egg, smoothing any melted chocolate around the middle to seal.

Return the whole eggs to the moulds to hold them upright and chill in the fridge until fully set.

VALENTINE'S BARK

As I have mentioned before, I often give food as homemade gifts – it's the thought that goes into your baking that counts and the fact that you spent time making them. This tasty chocolate Valentine's Bark can be customised depending on who you are giving it to and their preferences and is so easy to make. I used a base mix of white chocolate, tinting some pink with an oil-based food colouring (non oil-based food colouring can cause the chocolate to split). You could even take it up a notch by using ruby chocolate instead for a glorious pop of pink. I used all things Valentine-coloured to decorate my bark, but you can switch it up for other celebratory times of year such as Christmas or Easter. Break the bark into large shards and package up in treat bags tied with ribbon or little boxes for extra cuteness.

MAKES: 15
PREP: 10 minutes
COOK: 5 minutes
SET: 2 hours
LASTS: 4–5+ days, in the fridge

300g white chocolate
¼ tsp oil-based pink food colouring
25g mini marshmallows
75g red/pink sugar-coated chocolate beans (I use Smarties)
10g freeze-dried raspberries
75g red/pink sweets

Line a large rectangular baking tray (23 x 33cm) with parchment paper.

In a small heatproof bowl, break the white chocolate into pieces and melt in the microwave in short bursts or over a pan of simmering water (bain-marie) until smooth.

Pour 100g of the melted white chocolate into a separate bowl and mix in the oil-based pink food colouring until combined.

Pour the remaining melted white chocolate into the tray and spread out evenly to about 1cm thick. Drizzle the pink chocolate over the top and use the end of a cake skewer to swirl the chocolate together, creating a marbled pattern.

Scatter over the mini marshmallows, red/pink sugar-coated chocolate beans, freeze-dried raspberries and other red/pink sweets and chill in the fridge for 2 hours until set.

Cut or break into around 15 shards and enjoy.

CHOCOLATE DIPPY EGGS

We all enjoy dippy eggs and soldiers. Or at least I know that I spent my childhood eating soft-boiled eggs with runny yolks, dipping my slices of toast in and devouring. It is still one of my favourite things to eat, however, why not transform traditional dippy eggs into something that's fun to eat, indulgent and a little bit different? Use a shop-bought small hollow chocolate egg with the top chopped off, fill with this luxurious homemade chocolate sauce and serve with sticks of toasted hot cross buns for dipping. The ultimate Easter morning breakfast.

MAKES: 10–12
PREP: 30 minutes
COOK: 10 minutes
COOL: 30 minutes
LASTS: 1–2+ days, in the fridge

100g dark chocolate
100g milk chocolate
75ml double cream
75ml full-fat milk
30g golden syrup
1 tsp vanilla extract
10–12 hollow chocolate eggs
Hot cross buns, toasted (try my Homemade Hot Cross Buns, page 223)

In a heavy-based pan, break up the dark chocolate and milk chocolate into small pieces. Add the double cream, milk, golden syrup and vanilla extract and heat over a low-medium heat, stirring regularly. Once melted, leave the mixture to cool. Whisk every now and again to prevent a skin forming on the chocolate sauce.

While the mixture is cooling, carefully cut the tops off the chocolate eggs. I use a small sharp knife and carefully cut them off, avoiding cracking the shells.

Once the chocolate mixture has cooled, pour carefully into the shells. Make sure the shells are supported so they don't fall over and spill!

Toast some hot cross buns and cut into fingers – dip into the shells and enjoy a gooey chocolate DELICIOUS treat!

PANCAKES

We all appreciate a decent breakfast, don't we? Whether it's a bowl of cereal, something savoury or yoghurt and fruit, the choices are endless. However, my ultimate breakfast is pancakes – so much the better if they are served on pancake day or for a special birthday breakfast. I wanted to give you my fail-safe fluffy pancake recipe that you can make and enjoy whenever, and top with whatever you want. I topped mine with berries and a drizzle here because that's my favourite way to serve them, but you could serve with a slathering of speculoos (I use Biscoff), a chocolate spread (I use Nutella) or anything else that takes your fancy. You could even try adding 200g chocolate chips to the pancake batter for the best breakfast of them all!

SERVES: 6
PREP: 10 minutes
COOK: 10 minutes
LASTS: Best served fresh

275g self-raising flour
65g caster sugar
Pinch of salt
2 eggs
350ml full-fat milk
1 tsp vanilla extract
Vegetable oil

To Serve

Fruit
Caramel/chocolate drizzle

In a large bowl, mix the flour, sugar and salt together.

In a separate large bowl, whisk together the eggs, milk and vanilla extract. Add the liquid mixture to the dry mixture, then whisk until smooth.

Preheat a pan over a medium heat and rub a little vegetable oil over the base. Spoon a ladleful of the batter into the hot pan and cook on each side for 1–2 minutes or until you see bubbles on the surface of the pancake. Repeat until the batter is used up.

Serve however you like – I love fresh fruit and a caramel or chocolate drizzle.

GINGERBREAD MINCE PIES

The mince pie recipe on my blog is a classic festive bake and is so popular – ever since I posted it I have had endless requests for an alternative version with a twist. So I came up with the idea for these gingerbread mince pies – a homemade pastry with ground ginger and cinnamon for a wonderfully warming flavour, and a mincemeat studded with crystallised ginger and more. If you want to make your own mincemeat, you can find the recipe on my blog. These would go down well served at a festive party or celebration – why not give them a go? I promise they will become your new staple Christmas bake.

MAKES: 12
PREP: 1½ hours
BAKE: 15–20 minutes
COOL: 1 hour
LASTS: 2–3+ days, in the fridge

375g plain flour, plus extra for dusting
3 tsp ground ginger
1 tsp ground cinnamon
275g chilled unsalted butter, cubed, plus extra for greasing
125g caster sugar
1 egg, plus 1 beaten egg for brushing

Filling

600g mincemeat
75g crystallised ginger, finely chopped
1 tsp ground ginger
Zest of 1 lemon

Preheat the oven to 220°C/200°C fan. Grease and flour the inside of a 12-hole muffin tray.

Into a large bowl, sift the flour, ginger and cinnamon. Add the butter and rub the mixture together with your fingertips until it resembles breadcrumbs. Add the sugar and egg, mix and bring together with your hands. Knead in the bowl until smooth.

Turn the pastry out onto a lightly floured surface and roll out to 3–4mm thick. Use a 9cm round cutter to cut out 12 circles and press each carefully into a muffin tray hole.

Use a 7cm round cutter to cut out 12 circles from the remaining pastry (you may have to collect the scraps of pastry and re-roll after cutting the first batch of circles to have enough). Leave to one side for later.

Filling

In a large bowl, add the mincemeat, crystallised ginger, ground ginger and lemon zest and mix. Put a dollop of the mixture into each of the 12 muffin tray holes. Top each mince pie with the 7cm circles you cut out earlier, pressing the pastry lids into the pastry bases around the edges so that they are sealed.

If you have any leftover pastry, cut out some cute shapes. Brush a little beaten egg onto each mince pie and top with a shape.

Bake the mince pies in the oven for 15–20 minutes, or until lovely and golden in colour. Leave to cool in the tray for 10 minutes, before removing to cool fully.

CANDY CANES

Candy canes are probably the Christmas equivalent of autumnal toffee apples, right? Would you believe that these are easy to make and even better when homemade? Trust me. Candy canes have been one of the most requested Christmas treat recipes from my readers, because you all, just like me, want to have a go at making something fun and festive. The method is similar to making the peppermint cream recipe from my first book in the sense that it is a set icing sugar and egg white dough. Use other flavours if you don't fancy peppermint, but these canes are so good and too delicious to be hung on a Christmas tree.

MAKES: 15
PREP: 1 hour
SET: Overnight
LASTS: 7+ days, at room temperature

1 egg white
350–450g icing sugar, plus extra for dusting
1 tsp peppermint extract
½ tsp red food colouring

Line a baking tray with parchment paper.

Using a clean bowl and whisk (otherwise the egg white won't stiffen), add the egg white to the bowl and whisk until stiff peaks form. Add 350g of icing sugar and the peppermint extract and mix until a dough forms. Knead with your hands in the bowl until the dough is smooth – if it's still sticky, add the remaining 100g of icing sugar a little at a time until you reach a smooth dough.

Divide the dough into two and colour one batch red with the food colouring. Divide each batch into 15 small balls (30 balls in total).

On a work surface dusted with icing sugar, roll out one red ball and one uncoloured ball into thin sausage shapes about ½cm thick. Twist the two colours together and then turn at one end to make the hooked end of a candy cane shape. Repeat with the remaining balls.

Place onto the lined baking tray and leave to harden and set overnight at room temperature.

TOFFEE APPLES

I think we can all agree that toffee apples are one of the most autumnal and nostalgic treats to enjoy during Halloween and bonfire season. They are as fun to eat as they are sticky and any treat on a stick is cute! I find that although you can buy them in supermarkets, I am often not a fan of the toffee coating. Far better to make your own – the toffee is tastier and you can decorate them how you like. Use some Halloween-themed sprinkles to dip your toffee apples into or try chopped nuts or sugar-coated chocolates, or a mixture of all of them!

MAKES: 12
PREP: 1 hour
COOK: 30 minutes
COOL: 30 minutes
LASTS: 1–2+ days, in the fridge

12 small apples
Sprinkles (optional)
425g golden caster sugar
100ml water
1 tsp white wine vinegar
100g golden syrup

Line a large tray with parchment paper.

Put the apples in a large bowl and pour boiling water over them to remove any wax coating and help to make the toffee stick. Leave for about 1 minute. Drain the water, dry the apples well and stick a skewer into each one.

If using sprinkles, put some in a large, shallow bowl and set to one side.

In a large pan, add the sugar and water and heat over a low-medium heat until the sugar dissolves. Add the white wine vinegar and golden syrup and continue to heat until it reaches about 150°C (hard cracking stage). Use a sugar thermometer to monitor the temperature.

Remove the pan from the heat, and dip the apples in the toffee mixture, holding onto the skewers to avoid burning your fingers. Move the apples about in the pan to cover each one completely. Pull each apple up with the attached skewer and let the excess drips fall off before rolling the apple in the sprinkles to fully coat.

Place the apples carefully on the lined tray and leave to cool fully so that the toffee sets hard. Be careful – the toffee is EXTREMELY hot! If it's hardening in the pan while you are dipping the apples, gently reheat to help it loosen up again.

Afternoon Tea

MINI CUPCAKES

Cupcakes are one of the easiest things you can bake – they are always a crowd-pleaser and they are versatile enough to be adapted and served at any celebration. In cute mini form they are the perfect bite-sized treat for an afternoon tea. I like to bake these at Easter time or for birthday parties and I love to switch up the frosting and decorations depending on the event. I used a vanilla base, but you can make these chocolate by substituting 10g of the self-raising flour in the sponges with the same amount of cocoa powder, or replacing 15g of icing sugar in the frosting with the same amount of cocoa powder.

MAKES: 15

PREP: 15 minutes

BAKE: 11–13 minutes

COOL/DECORATE: 1 hour

LASTS: 2–3+ days, at room temperature

60g unsalted butter or baking spread

60g caster sugar

60g self-raising flour

1 egg

½ tsp vanilla extract

Buttercream

50g unsalted butter, at room temperature

100g icing sugar

½ tsp vanilla extract

Decoration

Sprinkles

Preheat the oven to 180°C/160°C fan and get 15 mini cupcake cases ready.

In a large bowl, beat the butter and sugar together until light and fluffy. Add the flour, egg and vanilla extract to the bowl and beat until smooth.

Divide the mixture equally between the 15 mini cupcake cases. Bake in the oven for 11–13 minutes. Remove and cool on a wire rack.

Buttercream

In a large bowl, beat the butter for a few minutes to loosen it. Add the icing sugar and vanilla extract and beat again until combined.

Decoration

Transfer the buttercream to a piping bag with your chosen piping nozzle fitted and pipe over the cupcakes. Scatter over some sprinkles.

LEMON MADELEINES

A madeleine is a classic French bake that not many people attempt themselves and I want to change that. I can't think of anything better than having a few of these shell-like sponges served alongside my afternoon tea or looking pretty on display at a birthday or summer party. They have a particularly light texture from whisking the eggs and adding a dash of leavening agent and with the fresh flavour of lemon, what's not to love? A dusting of icing sugar is the final flourish.

MAKES: 12
PREP: 30 minutes
BAKE: 9–10 minutes
COOL: 10 minutes
LASTS: Best served fresh

100g unsalted butter or baking
   spread, plus extra for
   greasing
2 eggs
100g caster sugar
100g plain flour, plus extra for
   dusting
½ tsp baking powder
Zest of 1 lemon
Icing sugar, for dusting
   (optional)

Preheat the oven to 200°C/180°C fan and use a pastry brush to brush a 12-hole madeleine tray with melted butter, and lightly dust with flour.

In a medium bowl, whisk the eggs and sugar until they are light and frothy. Add the flour, baking powder and lemon zest and whisk again until smooth. Chill in the fridge for 10 minutes.

Divide the mixture equally between the 12 holes, using 1 heaped tablespoon of mixture per madeleine. You do not need to spread the mixture out, just dollop in the middle of each madeleine mould.

Bake in the oven for 9–10 minutes, or until slightly golden in colour and the distinctive madeleine shape has formed. Transfer to a wire rack to cool a little, dust over some icing sugar (optional) and enjoy while still warm.

FLORENTINES

Florentines are quite an interesting bake, as you often see them displayed in the patisserie section and they seem posh and exclusive. But with a sweet biscuit-like pastry, lots of fruit and nuts and dipped into chocolate they are actually really yummy and a must for any occasion! The base is made of four simple ingredients – butter, sugar, golden syrup (you could use honey instead) and flour. It's then packed with all sorts, such as mixed nuts, candied peel and dried cranberries. Full of texture and flavour, the final dunk in melted chocolate finishes them off exquisitely. I reckon a little treat bag of these would make such a cute gift year-round!

MAKES: 20

PREP: 15 minutes

BAKE: 9–10 minutes

COOL/DECORATE: 2 hours

LASTS: 7+ days at room temperature

75g unsalted butter

75g soft light brown sugar

75g golden syrup

75g plain flour

50g candied peel

75g mixed nuts, chopped (I use pecans and almonds)

50g dried cranberries, chopped

250g milk or dark chocolate

Preheat the oven to 190°C/170°C fan and line three baking trays with parchment paper.

In a small pan, add the butter, sugar and golden syrup and heat gently until melted and combined.

In a large bowl, add the flour, candied peel, mixed nuts and dried cranberries. Pour in the butter mixture and stir until smooth.

Spoon 20 heaped teaspoonfuls of the mixture onto the lined baking trays, leaving a little space between each one for spreading during baking. Bake in the oven for 9–10 minutes until golden brown and even in colour. Leave to cool on the trays for at least 15 minutes, before cooling fully on a wire rack.

In a heatproof bowl, break up the milk or dark chocolate into pieces and melt in a microwave in short bursts or over a pan of simmering water (bain-marie) until smooth. Spread some of the melted chocolate onto the base of each florentine and return to the lined baking trays. Leave to set fully.

MINI CHOCOLATE LOAF CAKES

If you have followed my blog for a while you will know that I can't get enough of loaf cakes. Perhaps it's because they are simple to bake, easy to slice and store and always taste great. Baking them in miniature form just means I can eat more! These mini loaf cake cases are a cute size and are easy to find in most supermarkets. The chocolate sponge recipe couldn't be simpler, but topped with chocolate buttercream frosting and some chocolates these loaf cakes become something quite special. Honestly, take them to a party and you'll be everyone's friend!

MAKES: 12
PREP: 20 minutes
BAKE: 20–22 minutes
COOL/DECORATE: 2 hours
LASTS: 2–3 days, at room temperature

225g unsalted butter, at room emperature
225g soft light brown sugar
175g self-raising flour
50g cocoa powder
4 eggs
½ tsp vanilla extract

Buttercream

200g unsalted butter, at room temperature
350g icing sugar
50g cocoa powder
½ tsp vanilla extract

Decoration

Sprinkles
Chocolate sweets

Preheat the oven to 180°C/160°C fan and get 12 mini loaf cake cases ready.

In a large bowl, beat the butter and sugar together until light and fluffy. Add the flour, cocoa powder, eggs and vanilla extract and beat until the mixture is smooth.

Divide the mixture equally between the 12 mini loaf cake cases. Bake in the oven for 20–22 minutes. Remove and cool fully on a wire rack.

Buttercream

In a large bowl, beat the butter for a few minutes to loosen it. Add the icing sugar, cocoa powder and vanilla extract and beat again until combined. If the mixture is still a little thick after beating for about 5 minutes, add 1 tablespoon of boiling water to the mixture, beating well to create a smooth texture.

Decoration

Transfer the buttercream to a piping bag with a piping nozzle of your choice fitted and pipe over the cakes – I do swirly lines along the loaf cakes. Scatter over some sprinkles and some chocolate sweets.

MINI LEMON MERINGUE PIES

A lemon meringue pie is one of the most fresh and zingy bakes you can make and my classic recipe features on my blog, but for this book I wanted to improve it if I could and that's when I came up with individual Mini Lemon Meringue Pies. A homemade sweet shortcrust pastry (if you want to use shop-bought, that's totally fine), a tart and smooth lemon curd filling, topped with a light Italian meringue – three different textures that combine to create perfection. Italian meringue sounds intense, but use a thermometer to make it easier and you will enjoy the taste so much more than a normal meringue!

MAKES: 8
PREP: 2 hours
BAKE: 25 minutes
COOL/DECORATE:
2 hours
LASTS: 1–2+ days,
in the fridge

350g plain flour, plus extra for dusting
2 tbsp icing sugar
200g chilled unsalted butter, cubed, plus extra for greasing
2 egg yolks
2 tbsp cold water

see next page

Grease and dust flour over the insides of eight individual 10cm loose-bottomed tart tins.

In a large bowl, sift the flour and icing sugar and add the butter, egg yolks and cold water. Rub the mixture together with your fingertips until it resembles breadcrumbs, bring together with your hands and knead in the bowl until smooth.

Turn the pastry out onto a lightly floured work surface and roll out until 3mm thick. Cut out eight circles of pastry a little larger than the tart tins and press each pastry circle into the bottom and sides of each tin, trimming the edges. Chill in the fridge for 30 minutes.

Meanwhile, preheat the oven to 200°C/180°C fan. Cover each pastry case with a circle of parchment paper and fill each one with baking beans/rice. Bake 'blind' for 15 minutes.

Remove the parchment paper and the beans from each tin and bake for an extra 10 minutes or until the pastry is cooked through and turning golden in colour. Leave to cool in the tins.

Filling

Zest of 4 lemons

150ml lemon juice

100g unsalted butter, at room temperature

200g caster sugar

3 eggs

3 egg yolks

Topping

185g white granulated sugar

85ml water

95g egg whites

Filling

In a large pan, add the lemon zest, lemon juice, butter and sugar and heat, stirring until the mixture has dissolved and is smooth.

In a separate bowl, beat the eggs and egg yolks together and then add to the pan. Heat the mixture for 7–8 minutes until thickened. Add 1–2 tablespoons of the mixture to each pastry case.

Topping

In a heavy-based pan, add the sugar and water and bring to the boil, stirring occasionally with a wooden spoon. When the mixture starts to boil, monitor the temperature until it reaches 120°C (firm ball stage) with a sugar thermometer. If any sugar splashes up the sides of the pan while boiling, brush the sides with a pastry brush and cold water to stop the mixture crystallising.

Meanwhile, using a clean bowl and whisk (otherwise the egg whites won't stiffen), add the egg whites to the bowl and whisk until they start to form stiff peaks. When the sugar syrup has reached temperature, start to slowly trickle it onto the egg whites at the edge of the bowl while continuously whisking. Make sure you do this carefully so that the egg whites stay smooth.

Once all the sugar syrup has been added, continue to whisk the mixture fast and at high speed for 5–7 minutes until the mixture is smooth and has cooled down. Transfer the mixture to a piping bag and with a piping nozzle of your choice fitted, pipe onto the eight individual lemon meringue pies.

If you have a cook's blowtorch, carefully toast the edges of each meringue. Otherwise, place the meringues under the grill in the oven to brown slightly. Chill the lemon meringue pies for 1 hour. Remove them from the tins and enjoy.

HOT CROSS BUNS

I am 100% obsessed with hot cross buns and buy them all the time when they are in the shops, especially the fun and unusual flavours available at Easter time... but you can't beat the classics. You also can't beat anything homemade – yes it takes longer, but it is always worth the effort! I also find bread baking quite therapeutic – the kneading of the dough, the shaping of the buns, the anticipation while you wait for the dough to rise. I wrote this recipe to reflect my idea of the dream hot cross bun with a variety of spices and flavours, but you can switch them up however you want. Add chopped fruits or even chocolate chips to the dough for extra texture.

MAKES: 12
PREP: 30 minutes
BAKE: 20 minutes
PROVE: 2–3+ hours
LASTS: 1–2+ days,
at room temperature

225ml full-fat milk
500g strong white bread flour,
    plus extra for dusting
65g caster sugar
½ tsp salt
1 tsp ground cinnamon
½ tsp ground ginger
½ tsp ground nutmeg
Zest of 1 orange
7g dried yeast
50g chilled unsalted butter, cubed
2 eggs
200g raisins
Vegetable oil

Topping

30g strong white bread flour
30ml water
1 tbsp apricot jam

In a small pan, warm the milk until it's just about steaming. Leave to one side.

In a large bowl, add the flour, sugar, salt, cinnamon, ginger, nutmeg, orange zest and yeast. Add the butter and rub the mixture between your fingertips until it resembles breadcrumbs. Add the warmed milk, eggs and raisins and mix together. Knead for 5–10 minutes until the mixture is smooth, elastic and springy to touch.

Transfer the dough to a clean but lightly oiled bowl and cover with clingfilm. Leave to rise until doubled in size – this usually takes 1–2 hours. Once risen, turn out onto a floured work surface and knead lightly to 'knock it back'.

Preheat the oven to 200°C/180°C fan. Line a baking tray with parchment paper.

Divide the dough evenly into 12 balls (mine weighed 98g each) and place on the lined tray with a 1cm gap between them. Cover with a lightly oiled piece of clingfilm and leave for 45–60 minutes.

Topping

In a bowl, whisk the flour and water together and transfer to a piping bag with a piping nozzle fitted. Carefully pipe crosses over the dough balls. Bake in the oven for 20 minutes. Remove from the oven and use a pastry brush to lightly glaze each bun with apricot jam if you like them sticky and shiny. Leave to cool fully.

WELSH CAKES

Welsh cakes are unique and traditional – a warm Welsh cake topped with butter that starts to melt into it is irresistible to me. For those of you who have never eaten them, I would describe them as a mix between a scone and a pancake, with a touch of 'cookie' – sounds odd maybe, but try them before you decide. With a hint of mixed spice and currants running through them, these fragrant, griddled cakes may change your life!

MAKES: 15
PREP: 20 minutes
COOK: 20 minutes
COOL: 10 minutes
LASTS: 7+ days, at room temperature

250g plain flour, plus extra for dusting

100g caster sugar, plus 35g for dusting

½ tsp baking powder

½ tsp mixed spice

100g unsalted butter, cut into small pieces, plus 50g for frying

75g currants

1 egg, beaten

In a large bowl, add the flour, sugar, baking powder and mixed spice. Add the butter and rub the mixture together between your fingers until it resembles breadcrumbs. Add the currants and egg and bring together with a spatula at first and then your hand. Knead the dough lightly in the bowl to make sure it is smooth.

Turn out the dough onto a lightly floured work surface and roll out until 1cm thick. Using a round 6cm cutter, cut out the Welsh cakes – you will have to re-roll the mixture a couple of times to ensure you have enough dough.

Preheat a heavy-based frying pan or flat griddle pan to a medium heat. Grease with butter. Cook the Welsh cakes over a medium heat for about 3 minutes on each side until golden brown in colour. Be careful to rub off any excess butter and re-grease as you go so that the butter doesn't burn and ruin the Welsh cakes.

Once cooked, place the Welsh cakes onto a lined baking tray, and sprinkle on both sides with the extra sugar before serving.

CHOCOLATE ORANGE SCONES

Can you in all honesty have an afternoon tea without a scone? I don't think so – but whatever you think, a scone during the summer months can't be beaten. These beautiful scones are on a new flavour level, with a fragrant orange dough stuffed full of chocolate chunks (because we all know how much I adore a chocolate-orange combination!). It would be a crime not to top these with some clotted cream, but a chocolate to garnish makes these even more celebratory. If you don't like the orange flavour, you can leave it out or add lemon and white chocolate instead.

MAKES: 10–12
PREP: 30 minutes
BAKE: 10 minutes
COOL: 20 minutes
LASTS: 2+ days,
at room temperature

90g chilled unsalted butter, cubed

1 tsp baking powder

¼ tsp sea salt

350g self-raising flour, plus extra
   for dusting

50g caster sugar

50ml orange juice

125ml full-fat milk, warmed

Zest of 1 large orange

250g milk or dark chocolate
   chunks

1 egg, beaten

To Serve

Chocolate hazelnut spread
   (I use Nutella)

Clotted cream

Preheat the oven to 220°C/200°C fan. Line two baking trays with parchment paper and place in the oven to heat.

In a large bowl, add the butter, baking powder, sea salt and flour. Rub together between your fingertips until the mixture resembles breadcrumbs. Add the sugar, orange juice, milk and orange zest to the bowl. Stir with a spatula, as it will be very wet at first, and bring the dough together until it's smooth. Add the chocolate chunks to the dough, and fold through.

Turn the dough out onto a lightly floured work surface and roll it out or press it down until it is about 4–5cm thick. Using a round 5cm cutter, cut out the scones – you will have to re-roll the mixture a couple of times to ensure you have enough dough.

Remove the preheated trays from the oven and lay the scones onto them. Using a pastry brush, brush the tops of the scones with the beaten egg and bake in the oven for 10 minutes.

Leave to cool for about 20 minutes on the trays. Serve with chocolate spread and clotted cream.

JAM TARTS

When you have made your own jam, it seems appropriate to show it off and use it. That is where these delightful Jam Tarts come into play – sweet shortcrust pastry, homemade jam (page 236) and a sprinkling of creativity with the leftover pastry offcuts to decorate and you have a crowd-pleasing bake for adults and children alike. When I was younger one of my ultimate treats was a homemade jam tart with custard poured all over it – heaven! Have fun with the decoration or use any flavour jam you prefer to fill them.

MAKES: 8
PREP: 30 minutes
BAKE: 15–17 minutes
COOL: 1 hour
LASTS: 4–5+ days, at room temperature

350g plain flour, plus extra for dusting
2 tbsp icing sugar
200g chilled unsalted butter, cubed, plus extra for greasing
2 egg yolks
2 tbsp cold water

Filling

500–600g jam (any flavour of your choice – or try my homemade jam, page 236)

Topping

Spare pastry offcuts

Preheat the oven to 200°C/180°C fan. Grease and flour eight individual 10cm loose-bottomed tart tins.

In a large bowl, sift the flour and icing sugar, then add the butter, egg yolks and cold water. Rub the mixture together with your fingertips until it resembles breadcrumbs, bring together with your hands and knead in the bowl until smooth.

Turn the pastry out onto a lightly floured work surface and roll out until 3mm thick. Cut out eight circles of pastry a little larger than the tart tins and press each pastry circle into the bottom and sides of each tin, trimming the edges.

Filling

Add 1–2 tablespoons of jam filling to the middle of each of the pastry cases and spread out evenly.

Topping

If you have any leftover pastry offcuts, roll out and cut some strips or shapes to lay over the jam of each tart – I did hearts and star shapes! Bake the jam tarts in the oven for 15–17 minutes until the jam is bubbling and the pastry around the edges is golden in colour. Leave to cool in the tins for 10 minutes, then carefully remove the tarts and let them cool fully.

HEART MACARONS

Macarons are delicate and melt-in-the-mouth and especially impressive when served as part of an afternoon tea, but they can be a little intimidating to bake. I get it, there are a lot of mistakes that are easy to make when whipping up a batch of macarons, but once you have cracked the process there's no stopping you. My first book featured my classic macaron recipe, but for this book I wanted to make them extra special for Valentine's Day, so I came up with these Heart Macarons. Use a small piping nozzle to pipe these into shape or trace out some heart shapes onto your parchment paper first as a guide. Get creative and switch to any other shape, colour or even flavouring for other celebrations throughout the year.

MAKES: 25
PREP: 1 hour
BAKE: 16–20 minutes
FILL: 1 hour
LASTS: 3+ days, in the fridge

200g icing sugar
100g ground almonds
100g egg whites (about 3 eggs)
75g caster sugar
½ tsp red food colouring
Small pink sprinkles

Filling

50g unsalted butter, at room temperature
100g icing sugar
½ tsp red food colouring

Line three baking trays with parchment paper and leave to one side.

In a food processor, blitz the icing sugar and ground almonds together for 2 minutes on a high speed. Sieve into a large bowl and leave to one side – it's VERY important to sieve the mix and discard any lumps.

Using a clean bowl and whisk (otherwise the egg whites won't stiffen), add the egg whites to the bowl and whisk until thick and foamy. Gradually add the caster sugar 1 teaspoon at a time, whisking after each addition until all the sugar has been incorporated. Continue to whisk for 1–2 minutes, then add the red food colouring and whisk for 3–4 minutes until smooth and light.

Gently fold the egg white mixture into the icing sugar/ground almond mixture until well combined. Carefully 'wipe' the mixture around the edges of the bowl with a spatula a few times – in French, this is called 'macaronage'. When you lift the spatula out of the bowl, the mixture should be quite liquid in texture and form a V shape as it drops off the spatula.

Transfer the macaron mixture to a piping bag with a small round piping nozzle fitted and pipe the mixture either onto a macaron mat, or the lined baking trays. I pipe heart shapes, leaving them spaced at least 2–3cm apart from each other. Tap the trays onto the work surface several times to knock out any remaining air bubbles and sprinkle over the pink sprinkles. Leave the macarons to one side for 1 hour so that a skin is formed – this stage is important.

Meanwhile, preheat the oven to 150°C/130°C fan and bake the macarons for 16–20 minutes until they have risen to their 'feet' and are starting to peel away from the tray – leave to cool fully before removing the macaron shells carefully and lining them up, ready to be filled!

Filling

In a bowl, cream the butter and sugar together until smooth and supple and add the red food colouring to get a pink colour!

Transfer the mixture to a piping bag with a piping nozzle fitted. Pipe or spread some of the filling onto half of the macaron shells and sandwich together with the remaining shells.

HOMEMADE JAM

Jam is one of those versatile foods that is used so much for baking, slathered on toast at breakfast, or enjoyed simply as a jam sandwich. Why not make your own? I often make batches of my own jam to spread on top of my scones or sandwich between layers of my cakes. This beauty of a recipe is a strawberry-based jam, but you can use any berry you like or a combination of berries – just make sure you have the weight quantities correct. If you prefer to make a smaller batch, halve the quantity given in the recipe. If you don't have a thermometer for the jam, you can test as you cook it by adding a small dollop to a plate and freezing for a few minutes. If it freezes to a gel-like consistency, then it's ready.

**MAKES: 1kg
(2 x 500ml jars)**

PREP: 15 minutes

COOK: 30 minutes

COOL: 2 hours

LASTS: 3+ months, at room temperature, if not opened. 1 week in the fridge once opened.

1kg berries (I used strawberries)

800g caster sugar

75ml lemon juice

Zest of 1 lemon

Remove the tops of the strawberries with a sharp knife and give them a wash. Chop into quarters.

In a large pan, add the prepared strawberries and squash with a potato masher to soften and break down. Add the sugar, lemon juice and zest. Stir continuously over a low-medium heat so that the sugar dissolves into the fruit and lemon. Once dissolved, increase the heat to high and start to boil the mixture. Skim off any sediment that forms on the top of the jam as it boils and discard.

Using a sugar thermometer and stirring frequently, heat the mixture until it reaches 105°C.

Pour the jam very carefully into two warmed 500ml sterilised jam jars (the jars should be warmed so that they don't break as you pour in the boiling jam).

Seal the jars with sterilised lids while still warm and leave to cool completely.

PASSION FRUIT CURD

Passion fruit is one of the best fruits in the world – I love the contrast of its sweet but sharp taste and it's delicious as a cocktail ingredient or used in a bake. However, it's my Passion Fruit Curd that is out of this world amazing! I always use fresh passion fruit when making this curd and I don't bother removing the seeds. This recipe is cooked just like lemon curd and can be served in a similar way too. It's a great addition to any bake or served as a spread at afternoon tea. Try making it in a bain-marie, or in the microwave – the choice is yours!

MAKES: 700g (2 x 350ml jars)

PREP: 15 minutes

COOK: 30 minutes

COOL: 2 hours

LASTS: 3+ months, at room temperature, if not opened. 1 week in the fridge once opened.

In a large bowl, add the passion fruit pulp, lemon juice and sugar. Stir the mixture together, put the bowl over a pan of simmering water and add the butter. Let the butter melt. Pour the egg yolks into the passion fruit mixture and continue to heat, whisking continuously for 10–15 minutes until thickened. Alternatively, add all the ingredients to a large bowl, and microwave in 30-second bursts, stirring well each time until thickened. Set the curd mixture to one side to cool completely, stirring occasionally as it cools. Once cooled, pour into two sterilised 500ml jars and seal with sterilised lids.

200g passion fruit pulp
  (about 7–8 passion fruit)
65ml lemon juice
100g caster sugar
175g unsalted butter
9 egg yolks

Savoury, Bread and Pastry

MINI PARTY SAUSAGE ROLLS

Even though I only recently added this savoury bake to my blog, these beauties have been insanely popular and 100% deserve a place in this book. I have always loved a mini sausage roll and as the name suggests, they're great for a party! The charm of these is that you can prep them in advance, freeze and then bake just before your event. I flavour the sausagemeat with some simple but delicious spices for the best results – I hope you love them as much as I do.

MAKES: 24
PREP: 30 minutes
BAKE: 28–32 minutes
COOL: 10+ minutes
LASTS: 3 days, in the fridge

400g sausagemeat
2 garlic cloves, crushed
¼ tsp chilli flakes (optional)
1 tsp mixed herbs
Pinch of salt and pepper
65ml water
Plain flour, for dusting
350g ready-made puff pastry
1 egg, beaten

Preheat the oven to 210°C/190°C fan and line two large baking trays with parchment paper.

In a large bowl, add the sausagemeat, garlic, chilli flakes, mixed herbs, salt and pepper and the water and mix together. Alternatively, add to a food processor and blitz together until smooth and combined.

On a lightly floured work surface, roll out the pastry into a rectangle until it is about 35 x 23cm in size and cut down the middle to give two long lengths. Spread half of the sausagemeat mixture 1cm in from one of the long edges along one length of the pastry. Repeat with the other half of the sausagemeat and pastry. Fold the pastry over on each strip, covering the sausagemeat with pastry. Seal where the pastry meets, using a pastry brush dipped in the beaten egg. Once both lengths of pastry are rolled and sealed, cut each roll into 12 pieces (24 in total).

Place the sausage rolls onto the lined baking trays, with each sitting on the sealed side of the pastry. Brush the top of each sausage roll with more beaten egg and bake in the oven for 28–32 minutes until the pastry has puffed up nicely and the meat has cooked through.

Cool for 10 minutes and then enjoy hot, or cool completely and enjoy chilled straight from the fridge.

GARLIC STUFFED BREAD

You know when you make a recipe, and it says one garlic clove for the entire dish? Are you like me and at least double, if not triple the quantity? Well, you will definitely enjoy this Garlic-Stuffed Bread then. I used four garlic cloves, but you could increase the number of cloves if you want – the balance of the garlicky goodness with the crunch of the sea salt and the fresh parsley is spot on. Grabbing a bread loaf from any supermarket bakery, slicing it to create a pull-apart-style bake and packing it with the garlic butter is simple. The thing that turns it up a notch? All of the mozzarella that is stuffed into it!

SERVES: 12+
PREP: 15 minutes
BAKE: 30 minutes
COOL: 20 minutes
LASTS: 1–2 days (but best served fresh)

100g unsalted butter
4 garlic cloves, crushed
1 tsp sea salt
10g fresh parsley, finely chopped
1 large crusty bread loaf
250g mozzarella, grated

Preheat the oven to 200°C/180°C fan and line a large baking tray with parchment paper.

In a small bowl, add the butter, garlic and sea salt and microwave in short bursts until melted and smooth. Stir in the parsley.

On a chopping board, cut 2–5cm-sized diamonds into the top of the bread, cutting down only two-thirds into the loaf so that the base stays whole. Cut diagonals in one direction, then turn the bread around and cut in the other direction.

Carefully spoon the melted garlic butter mixture into the segments you have created and then sprinkle over the mozzarella, stuffing it into the cracks. Wrap the bread in foil and bake in the oven for 20 minutes.

Remove the foil and bake for another 10 minutes until the cheese browns and turns crispy.

Let the bread cool for 20 minutes and then enjoy.

HOMEMADE CRUMPETS

Just like a Welsh Cake (page 226) I am always up for a hot fresh crumpet, with a slathering of butter melting on top. I know you might be asking, 'Why would I bother making crumpets?', but honestly, they are so much easier than you think and also kinda fun to watch as they cook because of the bubbles that form on their surface. I make my crumpets, and then toast them immediately for crumpet perfection, but if you have more patience than me, you can freeze them and toast separately when you're in the mood for one. Homemade crumpets are far tastier than the shop-bought versions, and I would highly recommend you give them a go.

MAKES: 8
PREP: 30 minutes
PROVE: 20 minutes
COOK: 15 minutes
COOL: 30 minutes
LASTS: 2–3 days

175g plain flour
225ml warm water
½ tsp sea salt
1 tsp baking powder
Pinch of caster sugar
5g dried yeast
25g unsalted butter, at room
   temperature, for greasing

In a large bowl, add the flour, warm water and sea salt and whisk together for 1–2 minutes. Add the baking powder, sugar and yeast and whisk for another minute. Cover the bowl with clingfilm and leave the mixture to sit in a warm place for 20 minutes.

Place a large flat frying pan over a medium-high heat. Grease three or four 9cm crumpet rings with the butter and place the rings onto the pan.

Ladle crumpet batter into the rings so that they are half full. Heat at medium-high heat (level 7/9 on my hob) for 1½ minutes, and then reduce the heat to medium-low (level 4/9) and cook for a further 3–4 minutes. During the cooking time, bubbles should appear on the surface of the crumpets and they should start to come away from the edges of the rings.

Remove the rings carefully, flip the crumpets over and cook for another 30 seconds before removing from the pan. Leave to cool.

To serve, toast the crumpets for 2–3 minutes, spread on some butter and enjoy.

HOMEMADE PRETZELS

Have you ever eaten a fresh and still warm salty pretzel? They are indescribably good – a freshly made bread dough, sprinkled with chunks of sea salt is a tasty snack. Pretzels are a little weird to make, as they are similar to bagels in the sense that you have to boil them in water for a bit before baking. Although a little time-consuming, it is 100% worth it. If you want to try a sweet version, dunk the pretzels in some cinnamon sugar once baked – life changing!

MAKES: 8
PREP: 45 minutes
PROVE: 15 minutes
COOK: 10+ 15 minutes
COOL: 30 minutes
LASTS: 1–2+ days

350ml warm water

7g dried yeast

1 tsp sea salt, plus extra for sprinkling

15g caster sugar

25g unsalted butter, melted

600–700g plain flour, plus extra for dusting

2L water

125g bicarbonate of soda

In a large bowl, add the warm water and yeast, whisk together and leave to sit for a minute or two. Add the sea salt, sugar and butter to the bowl and whisk again to combine – it may look a little weird. Add the flour, 200g at a time, mixing with a spatula between each addition until you have added 600g of flour. If the mixture still feels sticky, slowly add more flour until the dough is smooth and springs back when touched.

Turn out the dough onto a lightly floured work surface and knead for 5 minutes until you have a smooth round ball of dough. Put the dough into a lightly oiled bowl and leave to rest for 15 minutes.

Meanwhile, preheat the oven to 210°C/190°C fan and line two baking trays with parchment paper. In a large pan, pour the water and add the bicarbonate of soda – bring to the boil.

Remove 125g portions of dough from the rested dough and on a very lightly floured surface, roll each portion of dough into a long sausage shape, about 60cm long. Make the pretzel shape by forming a circle with the middle section of each sausage, crossing it over and bringing each length down to meet the circle again.

Once the water is boiling, drop the pretzels into the pan, one or two at a time so you don't overcrowd them, and boil each for 30 seconds. Remove with a slotted spoon and drain off as much water as possible before placing them onto the lined baking trays. Sprinkle each pretzel with chunky sea salt and bake for 15 minutes until golden brown in colour and delicious. Leave to cool for 30 minutes on the trays and enjoy.

CHEESE PESTO WHIRLS

One of the most classic savoury bakes in the world is cheese straws – there is just something about them that is amazing. Pastry and cheese together is always warming and delightful, but whack in a load of pesto and they are instantly better. Instead of straw shapes, I decided to give you my recipe for Cheese Pesto Whirls, an ideal snack for any celebration or refined enough to be served as a little starter. I use red pesto, but use green if you prefer or you can even make your own using the recipe in this book (page 258).

MAKES: 16
PREP: 30 minutes
BAKE: 12–14 minutes
CHILL: 30 minutes
COOL: 15+ minutes
LASTS: 2–3+ days, in the fridge

Plain flour, for dusting
350g ready-made puff pastry
40g red pesto
50g Parmesan, finely grated
100g mature Cheddar cheese,
  finely grated

Preheat the oven to 220°C/200°C fan and line two large trays with parchment paper.

On a lightly floured work surface, roll out the pastry into a large rectangle until it is 3–4mm thick. Spread the red pesto evenly onto the pastry. Sprinkle the Parmesan and Cheddar onto the pesto and press down slightly.

From long side to long side, roll up the pastry tightly into a long sausage shape. If the pastry is a bit soft by this point, chill in the fridge for 30 minutes.

Remove and slice the pastry sausage into 1cm-wide slices with a sharp knife to form the cheese pesto whirls and lay onto the lined baking trays. Bake in the oven for 12–14 minutes until golden brown in colour. Leave to cool for 15 minutes and enjoy warm or leave to cool fully and enjoy them cold.

BACON CHEESE STRAWS

As I decided to include my Cheese Pesto Whirls recipe (page 248) in this book without shaping them into the traditional straws, I thought it only right to use the straw method elsewhere, and here it is! A sheet of puff pastry, a little mustard, streaky bacon and a load of cheese... so simple and yet so tasty. These are fun to make with your kids, as it can get a little messy with the cheese falling out, but that is part of their charm. I love to serve these when I have friends over for drinks and snacks, but they are also easy to transport to a birthday party. Equally delicious served warm or chilled, make them ahead of time if you prefer.

MAKES: 14
PREP: 30 minutes
BAKE: 22–26 minutes
CHILL: 30 minutes
COOL: 15+ minutes
LASTS: 2–3+ days, in the fridge

Plain flour, for dusting
350g ready-made puff pastry
1 tbsp Dijon mustard
100g mature Cheddar cheese, grated
14 slices streaky bacon
Pinch of pepper
1 egg, beaten

Preheat the oven to 220°C/200°C fan and line two large trays with parchment paper.

On a lightly floured work surface, roll out the pastry into a large rectangle until 3–4mm thick. Spread the mustard evenly onto the pastry. Sprinkle the cheese onto the mustard and press down slightly. Lay the slices of bacon on top of the cheese, from long side to long side, leaving a small thin gap between each piece so there is room to cut. Sprinkle over some pepper.

Slice into strips with a sharp knife, using the gaps between the bacon as your guide. Twist each strip 4–5 times to create twisted straws and place onto the lined baking trays. Chill in the fridge for 30 minutes.

Using a pastry brush, brush the exposed pastry of each straw with the beaten egg. Bake in the oven for 22–26 minutes until golden brown in colour and the bacon is cooked through. Leave to cool for 15 minutes and enjoy warm or cool fully and enjoy them cold.

SPICY CHICKEN ROLLS

I've already included a recipe for Mini Party Sausage Rolls (page 240) in this book, but these Spicy Chicken Rolls are a delicious alternative! I find it so much easier to mince my chicken meat in a food processor and then whack all the other ingredients in with it so that the mixture is evenly seasoned and spiced. The spice is optional, but amazing – you can reduce the heat by using mild chilli powder instead of the chilli flakes, or leave the chilli flakes out completely – but personally, I think they taste insane as they are.

MAKES: 30
PREP: 30 minutes
BAKE: 20–23 minutes
COOL: 10+ minutes
LASTS: 3 days, in the fridge

500g chicken breasts
2 tsp chilli powder
2 garlic cloves
1 tsp onion powder
1 tsp mixed herbs
1 tsp smoked paprika, plus extra for dusting
½ tsp chilli flakes
½ tsp ground cumin
Pinch of salt and pepper
75g mature Cheddar cheese, grated
50ml cold water
Plain flour, for dusting
350g ready-made puff pastry
1 egg, beaten

Preheat the oven to 210°C/190°C fan and line two large baking trays with parchment paper.

In a food processor, add the chicken breasts, chilli powder, garlic, onion powder, mixed herbs, smoked paprika, chilli flakes, cumin, salt and pepper, cheese and cold water. Blitz the mixture together until smooth and combined.

On a lightly floured work surface, roll out the pastry into a large rectangle until it is about 35 x 23cm in size and cut down the middle into two long lengths. Spread half of the chicken mixture onto one long length, about 1cm in from one of the long edges. Repeat this with the other half of the mixture and the other pastry half. Fold the pastry over on each half, covering the spiced chicken meat with pastry and letting the excess pastry meet at the top. Seal these two edges of the pastry together with some of the beaten egg. Then press a fork along to seal more securely and make a pattern.

Using a sharp knife, cut each long spicy chicken roll into 15 pieces (30 in total). Place onto the lined baking trays, brush the top of each spicy chicken roll with more of the beaten egg and add a small sprinkle of smoked paprika to each. Bake in the oven for 20–23 minutes until the pastry has puffed up nicely and the meat has cooked through. Leave to cool for 10 minutes on the trays and enjoy hot or cool completely and enjoy chilled from the fridge.

SCOTCH EGGS

We have all seen shop-bought scotch eggs included in a picnic spread and we can all appreciate the bite-sized ones at a party – pre-dinner snack anyone? But a freshly made scotch egg, full size, with a gooey centre, oh my actual days! Yes, I know you have to commit to frying the scotch eggs, but follow the temperatures in the recipe and you will see that barely any oil absorbs into them once cooked. The sausagemeat mix is easy to make, the egg yolks can be made runny or not depending on how you like them and you can change up the spices as you wish. They're SO GOOD!

MAKES: 4
PREP: 1 hour
COOK: 20 minutes
COOL: 30+ minutes
LASTS: 2–3 days, in the fridge

4 medium eggs
500g sausagemeat
35g stuffing mix
1 tsp chopped parsley
1 tsp chopped thyme
½ tsp mixed herbs
¼ tsp chilli flakes
Pinch of salt and pepper
75g plain flour
1 egg, beaten
75g dried breadcrumbs
1L sunflower oil

Bring a medium pan of water to the boil, then carefully lower the four eggs into the pan with a slotted spoon. Simmer the eggs for 6 minutes for a soft-boiled scotch egg, or 7½ minutes for a hard-boiled scotch egg.

Meanwhile, prepare a bowl of iced water to carefully drop the eggs into once boiled, so that they cool immediately and stop cooking. Slightly crack the shells of the eggs at this stage as you transfer them to the iced water so that they are easier to peel once fully cooled.

In a separate large bowl, add the sausagemeat, stuffing mix, parsley, thyme, mixed herbs, chilli flakes and the salt and pepper. Mix together until well combined.

Carefully peel the shell off the eggs. Portion the sausagemeat into four equal pieces (about 115g each). Using a piece of clingfilm, take one portion and flatten it down on the clingfilm into a circular shape. Add a peeled and cooled egg to the middle of the sausagemeat and use the clingfilm to help bring the sides up and around, wrapping the egg fully in sausagemeat. Repeat for each egg.

Lay out three separate bowls and add the flour to one, the beaten egg to one and the breadcrumbs to one. Roll each scotch egg in flour, then egg and finally into the breadcrumbs so they are fully coated. Put onto a plate and reserve to one side for later.

In a large pan, add the oil – I used 1 litre in a wide pan, so I could fit two scotch eggs in at a time. The oil needs to be 5–6cm deep. Heat the oil to 160°C – use a digital thermometer to check the temperature. Any colder and the oil may soak into the scotch eggs, any hotter and you risk burning them. Once at temperature, carefully lower the scotch eggs into the oil and fry for 9–10 minutes, turning halfway through until crispy and golden. Remove carefully with a slotted spoon onto kitchen paper to drain away the excess oil. Leave to cool for 30 minutes and enjoy warm or leave to cool fully and chill in the fridge before serving.

VEGETABLE TARTS

Puff pastry tarts are one of the most versatile bakes you can make. They work as a starter, as a main for dinner, as a lunch or even a snack and they are insanely easy to put together. I buy ready-made puff pastry, roll it out and portion it into the number of tarts I want to make (six for this recipe). Top the tarts with whatever ingredients you prefer. I used a homemade pesto for these (the recipe makes more then you need, but the leftovers are great for many other things) and then used a variety of my most beloved toppings. Have fun with them, experiment and enjoy!

MAKES: 6
PREP: 30 minutes
COOK: 18–22 minutes
COOL: 10 minutes
LASTS: 2 days in the fridge (but best served fresh)

Pesto

60g basil leaves
60g pine nuts
30g Parmesan
Pinch of salt and pepper
50–60ml olive oil

Tarts

350g ready-made puff pastry
6 tsp pesto (above)
3 tsp sun-dried tomato paste
10 asparagus, chopped
1 red pepper, sliced
12 cherry tomatoes, chopped
75g feta cheese
75g mature Cheddar cheese, grated

Pesto

In a food processor, add the basil, pine nuts, Parmesan and salt and pepper. Blitz the mixture until broken down. Continue to mix, drizzling in the olive oil continuously until you reach the consistency of pesto you want – I like mine quite wet.

Store the pesto in the fridge in a sealed container – leftover pesto lasts for one week in the fridge.

Tarts

Preheat the oven to 210°C/190°C fan and line two large trays with parchment paper.

Roll the puff pastry into a rectangle about 35 x 23cm in size, and cut into six squares. Put three squares onto each baking tray, leaving space between each square to allow for spreading during baking. Using a sharp knife, score around the edges of each square to form a border on the pastry.

Spread 1 teaspoon of homemade pesto and ½ teaspoon of sun-dried tomato paste onto each pastry square, inside the scored border. Scatter over the asparagus, red pepper and tomatoes. Crumble over the feta and sprinkle over the Cheddar. Bake the tarts in the oven for 18–22 minutes until the pastry is cooked and golden in colour. Leave to cool for 10 minutes.

HAM, LEEK & MUSHROOM QUICHE

I find that a quiche is one of those bakes that lends itself well to lunchtime, dinnertime or even as part of a mid-afternoon snack. Delightfully full of flavour, the pastry base from this recipe is so easy to make at home, but there is no shame in using shop-bought pastry to save on time. The filling is a breeze to put together – cook off the leeks and mushrooms slightly before adding all the layers to the pastry and pouring over the eggy mixture before baking.

SERVES: 12
PREP: 1 hour
COOK: 50 minutes
COOL: 1 hour
LASTS: 2–3+ days in the fridge

265g plain flour, plus extra for dusting

115g chilled unsalted butter, cubed, plus extra for greasing

Pinch of salt

2 tbsp cold water

Filling

2 medium leeks, sliced into 1cm rounds

150g mushrooms, chopped into quarters

200g ham, chopped

250g mature Cheddar cheese

100ml double cream

2 eggs

Salt and pepper, to taste

In a large bowl, add the flour, butter and salt and rub together with your fingertips until the mixture resembles breadcrumbs. Add the cold water, 1 tablespoon at a time, kneading the dough after each addition to bring the dough together. Knead the dough until smooth, wrap in clingfilm and chill in the fridge for 30 minutes.

Meanwhile, preheat the oven to 200°C/180°C fan and grease and flour a loose-bottomed 23cm tart tin.

Turn the dough out onto a lightly floured work surface and roll out until it is 3–4mm thick. Press the pastry into the base and sides of the tart tin and cut away any excess. Add a circle of parchment paper to the tart tin and fill with baking beans/rice. Bake the pastry 'blind' in the oven for 20 minutes. Remove the parchment paper and beans and bake for a further 5 minutes. Leave to cool in the tin.

Filling

Lightly grease a medium pan with butter, add the leeks and mushrooms and cook over a medium heat for a few minutes until the leeks have softened and the mushrooms have cooked slightly.

Sprinkle the ham and half of the cheese onto the base of the tart case. Add the leeks and mushrooms on top.

In a bowl, whisk the double cream, eggs and salt and pepper together until combined. Pour into the tart tin, then sprinkle over the rest of the cheese. Bake the quiche in the oven for 20–23 minutes, or until there is a slight wobble in the middle and the pastry has browned a little. Leave to cool, and then remove from the tart tin.

GRANARY BREAD

I adore baking bread at home and it's one of the best smells of all wafting through the house. Enjoying a sandwich or a slice of toast made with a homemade granary loaf just can't be beaten. I like to use a mix of white bread flour and wholemeal bread flour for this loaf because it creates a lovely balance of flavours, especially with the sweetness from a touch of honey. Feel free to use all white bread flour for a pure white bread loaf or all wholemeal flour for a more wholesome flavour – it's up to you!

SERVES: 10
PREP: 2 hours
PROVE: 2+ hours
BAKE: 35–40+ minutes
COOL: 1 hour
LASTS: 1–2 days (but best served fresh)

Vegetable oil
250g strong white bread flour
250g strong wholemeal bread flour
7g dried yeast
1 tsp sea salt
2 tbsp olive oil
1 tbsp honey
300ml warm water

Lightly oil a 900g loaf tin.

In a large bowl, add the strong white bread flour and strong wholemeal bread flour. On one side of the bowl, add the yeast and on the other side of the bowl add the sea salt. It's important to keep these separate so that the salt doesn't kill the live yeast.

Pour the olive oil, honey and 200ml of the warm water into the bowl and start to bring the dough together with a spatula. Start kneading and add the remaining 100ml water slowly (you may not need it at all!) until you have a smooth and malleable bread dough. It should spring back when touched.

Transfer the dough to the loaf tin, cover with a lightly oiled piece of clingfilm and leave in a warm place to rise until doubled in size – this may take about 2 hours.

Towards the end of the proving process, preheat the oven to 200ºC/180ºC fan. Bake the loaf in the oven for 35–40+ minutes until it has browned on top. When you remove the bread from the tin, it should make a hollow sound when you tap it on the bottom. Leave to cool fully and enjoy.

Index

Seasonal Index

Acknowledgements

My family… you have always shown me how much you believe in me, by looking after my pets when I have had to go away for work, dropping off ingredients at all hours, getting me a random light bulb when I am in the middle of working, and so much more. I know what I do is a bit hard to explain, but I cannot thank you enough for always supporting me while I do it.

My parents… you have supported me through so much. Whether it has been personally, with work, or whatever. I know how much you love me, and I cannot describe how much I love you guys too. I will always appreciate the care and encouragement you have given me.

My brother… thank you for getting me a load of baking ingredients when they were so hard to find, for the endless supply of coffee and syrups to keep me going. I promise that ONE DAY I will show up to the office with cake!

My friends… I know all I do is talk about work, but as you can tell, I think it's going to take a while for me to stop thinking these are all 'pinch me' moments. I cannot say thank you enough for helping me throughout all the really hard times, then being there to celebrate with me when it has gone well. For letting me rant when we go for coffee dates, dinners, drinks or whatever, THANK YOU.

To my JP team… Lily and Steph. Thank you. You guys have probably seen me at my highest and lowest, from crying on my kitchen floor to going out to celebrate good book news with cocktails. The adventure has only just begun, and I'm so happy to have you guys on that journey with me. I know I can trust you with every worry and concern I have and, despite you two jokingly bickering all the time, you are family and I love you so much.

Sam, Alice and Abby… I genuinely can't believe that I am writing these words right now – my

second book! Thank you for being the best little team and helping me create this entire new world of books. Thank you for letting me be myself and helping me grow. All of your kind words, your confidence in me and all of your amazing talents have helped me on this journey.

Thank you to everyone at Ebury for believing in me too. The fact that you trusted me so much with my vision, what I wanted and thought would work – and how it's turned into such an amazing series of books so far – means so much, you are the best publishers EVER!!

Ellis, Sarah, Maria, Julia and Hannah… you guys are the absolute dream. You brought this book to life, and I can't thank you enough. Ellis, you know how awkward I am when being photographed, so I appreciate your patience with my level of weird! Sarah, Maria and Julia, you guys are insane! You baked and made everything so perfectly that I can't say it enough. (Also, Sarah, sorry for the toffee apple situ!) Hannah, I am just obsessed with every look and prop you brought in because oh my days I want to have it all.

To my followers, I literally wouldn't be here without you. I wouldn't have had a first book, let alone a second, without every single one of you. You support every move I make within Jane's Patisserie; you shout about and bake every single recipe I post on my blog or publish in my books and you just really are the best followers ever.

Many of you who know me personally will know how much of a struggle my journey of blogging has been over the past couple of years. Various things in that time have made me feel like I wasn't good enough, so I just want to say thank you – thank you for putting up with all my panicking and worrying, and for helping me see that what I do is amazing, and that I should believe in myself.

Jane x

CONVERSION CHARTS

OVEN TEMPERATURES

110°C	90°C fan	225°F	Gas Mark ¼
130°C	110°C fan	250°F	Gas Mark ½
140°C	120°C fan	275°F	Gas Mark 1
150°C	130°C fan	300°F	Gas Mark 2
170°C	150°C fan	325°F	Gas Mark 3
180°C	160°C fan	350°F	Gas Mark 4
190°C	170°C fan	375°F	Gas Mark 5
200°C	180°C fan	400°F	Gas Mark 6
220°C	200°C fan	425°F	Gas Mark 7

WEIGHT CONVERSIONS (METRIC VS IMPERIAL)*

15g	½oz
25g	1oz
40g	1½oz
50g	2oz
75g	3oz
100g	4oz
150g	5oz
175g	6oz
200g	7oz
225g	8oz
250g	9oz
275g	10oz
350g	12oz
375g	13oz
400g	14oz
425g	15oz
450g	1lb
550g	1¼lb
675g	1½lb
900g	2lb
1.5kg	3lb

VOLUME CONVERSIONS (METRIC VS IMPERIAL)

25ml	1fl oz
50ml	2fl oz
85ml	3fl oz
150ml	5fl oz (¼ pint)
300ml	10fl oz (½ pint)
450ml	15fl oz (¾ pint)
600ml	1 pint
700ml	1¼ pints
900ml	1½ pints
1 litres	1¾ pints
1.2 litres	2 pints
1.25 litres	2¼ pints
1.5 litres	2½ pints
1.6 litres	2¾ pints
1.75 litres	3 pints
1.8 litres	3¼ pints
2 litres	3½ pints

*28.35g = 1oz but the measurements in this table have been rounded up or down to make conversions easier.

Published by Sourcebooks
P.O. Box 4410, Naperville, Illinois 60567-4410
(630) 961-3900
sourcebooks.com

Originally published in 2022 in Great Britain by Ebury Press, an imprint of
Ebury Publishing. Ebury Press is part of the Penguin Random House group of
companies whose addresses can be found at global.penguinrandomhouse.com

Cataloging-in-Publication Data is on file with the Library of Congress.

Printed and bound in China.
CCO 10 9 8 7 6 5 4 3 2 1

This book is made from Forest Stewardship Council® certified paper.